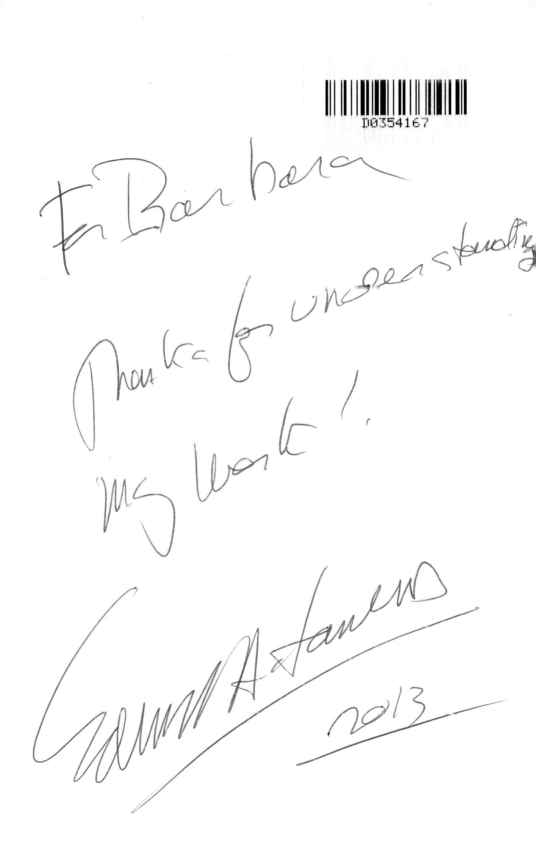

For Barbara

Thanks for understanding
my work!

2013

Managing YOUR STRESS in Today's World

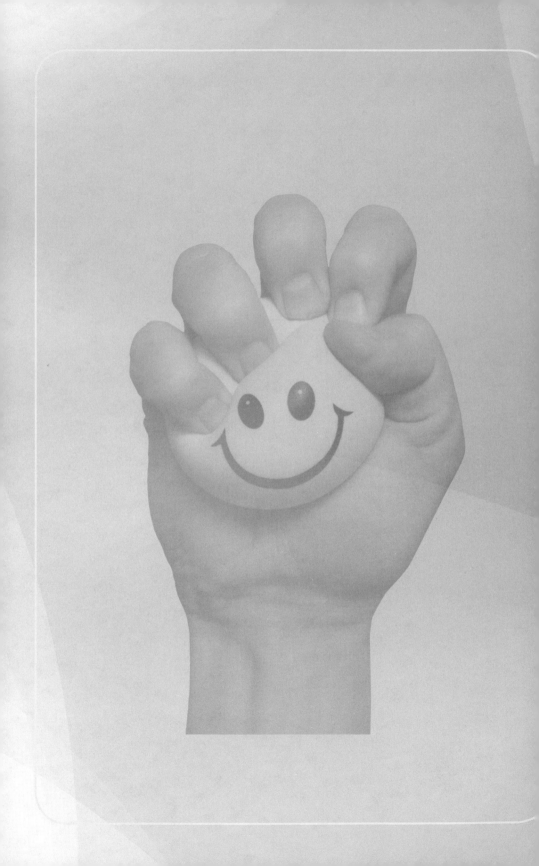

Managing YOUR STRESS

in Today's World

Edward A. Taub, M.D., FAAP

With Michael Levin
& David Oliphant

 **Reader's Digest** The Reader's Digest Association, Inc.
Pleasantville, NY / Montreal

To my brother, Lanny Taub, M.D., who reminds me that love is all there is.
—*Edward A. Taub, M.D., FAAP*

For Suzanne, Chynna, Walter, Isaac, and Aliya Levin.
—*Michael Levin*

To my partner in business and in life, Deborah A. Kalman. Thank you for always
being there for me in every way.
—*David Oliphant*

A READER'S DIGEST BOOK

@ 2009 Edward A. Taub, M.D., FAAP, Michael Levin, and David Oliphant
All rights reserved. Unauthorized reproduction, in any manner, is prohibited.

Reader's Digest is a registered trademark of The Reader's Digest Association, Inc.

A co-publishing venture with OK, Inc.

Library of Congress cataloging information is available on request.
ISBN 978-1-60652-127-4

Editorial Consultant: Deborah Kalman
Editorial Assistance: Dianne Barnum
Cover Designer: George McKeon
Interior Designer: Nick Anderson
Copy Editor: Barbara Booth
Cover and background images © iStockphoto®
Indexer: Andrea Chesman

READER'S DIGEST TRADE PUBLISHING
President & Publisher: Harold Clarke
Associate Publisher: Rosanne McManus
Executive Editor: Dolores York

THE READER'S DIGEST ASSOCIATION, INC.
President and Chief Executive Officer: Mary Berner
President, RD Community: Eva Dillon

Printed in the United States of America

1 3 5 7 9 10 8 6 4 2

NOTE TO OUR READERS
The contents of this book are a reflection of the authors' philosophy, beliefs, and clinical experience.
The information contained herein should not be substituted for, or used to alter, medical therapy without
consultation with your personal physician.

Start the day with love,

Fill the day with love,

End the day with love.

—SAI BABA

CONTENTS

Introduction   ix

CHAPTER 1   It's Still America   1

CHAPTER 2   What Is Stress, Anyway?   15

CHAPTER 3   Reconnecting with Our Families   27

CHAPTER 4   Good News: You Have More Control Than You Think   39

CHAPTER 5   Eating Right: Food for Thought   57

CHAPTER 6   Stress: It's about Time   69

CHAPTER 7   Looking for Love in All the Right Places   83

CHAPTER 8   Moving beyond Fear   93

CHAPTER 9   Harnessing the True Power of the Mind   105

CHAPTER 10   It's Still America, and You're Still You!   115

Epilogue: Dr. Taub's Emergency Stress Meditations   120

Index   123

Acknowledgments   128

INTRODUCTION

It's especially important to remember during this traumatic, virtually unparalleled time of economic crisis that health is our most important asset. After all, what good are those jobs, savings accounts, cars, and even the homes that so many Americans are concerned about right now if we don't have the good health to enjoy them?

These days, a wise physician recognizes that much of the disease and discomfort he or she is being asked to treat is somehow caused by stress. My purpose is to inform patients (and readers who don't want to become patients) that stress is now one of the major viruses of our times, affecting so many Americans and ruining the health and happiness of so many lives.

Stress is like the feeling of being stranded in a small boat with a broken mast and one broken oar, somewhere out in the ocean where you can barely see a dim outline of the shore, far from a safe haven or harbor. Just imagine the choices you are faced with. Thirsty and exhausted, you have two choices—stay where you are and wait for someone to find you before it is too late or do whatever is possible to reach the shore—using the oar, paddling with your hands, even swimming in the relatively warm, calm ocean.

So what will you do? Pray for help and wait? Or pray for help, gather your strength, and head toward shore using any possible means?

I'm writing to help you make the right choices for living in today's world by reaching out to your Guardian Angels. That's right; Guardian Angels. We all have Guardian Angels, which I realize is a stunning concept coming from a traditionally trained, mature, scientific physician. But the fact is, we've probably all experienced a time—perhaps when we are away from the day-to-day, out in nature or gazing at the stars—when we realize that in some way we are part of something much greater than ourselves. That moment of realization allows us to feel our Guardian Angels all around, helping us to heal and attain hope, peace, and love.

Our Guardian Angels are our connection to God; they are our divine intermediaries. So at both a scientific and spiritual level, my intention is to light up your brain's receptor cells to feel the presence of these angels, who will be able to help you in every aspect of your life, including recovery from the toxic effects of stress.

My own Guardian Angel is my mother, who died three years ago. I feel her presence all around me, all the time during this stressful time in my life when my younger brother, her only other child, is suffering from cancer. She is reminding me of what she taught my brother and me while she was alive, "Love is all there is." Usually our Guardian Angel is the person or persons in our memory who gave us the most love, care, warmth, hope, and peace. Defined this way, who are your Guardian Angels? In the following pages, you'll discover some new angels who are watching over you.

I'm not going to pull punches. Because so many Americans are being seriously harmed by stress in these extremely challenging times, my purpose is to help you preserve your health, which is still your most precious asset. My clinical goal is to help you manage your stress, especially today, and prevent you from getting stressed out in the future by shining the light of truth on the real causes of your stress. This is not an intellectual exercise, but rather a scientific and spiritual stress treatment for the bad economic times we are living in.

What makes these precarious times even more challenging is that the present medical care system often aggravates more than it helps to alleviate our stress problems. Here's why. The medical system in the United States takes a diagnosis and treatment–centered approach instead of focusing on preventive care. This results in a number of patients taking a lot of prescribed drugs, which leads to the issue of the unknown side effects of taking multiple prescription drugs.

In addition, medicine has undergone a radical restructuring. Today, doctors spend more and more of their time looking at computer screens rather than people. And you're lucky if you are able to see the same doctor on two consecutive visits. But it's not the doctors who are at fault. Doctors are as well trained, dedicated, and devoted to their patients as ever before. They still follow the credo, "First, do no harm." Yet, despite the fact that our nation has some of the best doctors in the world, our current health care system often acts as a drain on our physical, mental, and economic well-being, as we confront complex issues such as drug side effects and rising health care costs.

So if we can't always look to the medical community to help manage our stress, whom can we trust?

Ourselves.

And our Guardian Angels.

Let me show you how.

We usually think that if our circumstances are good, then we will automatically feel good. But that really isn't so, because people who are in horrible circumstances can feel at great peace, and people with wonderful circumstances in their lives can feel terrible. The actor Michael J. Fox, who has Parkinson's disease, is a good example of a person with a bad disease and a great attitude. A similarly upbeat patient of mine who also has a debilitating disease, says, "The only real handicap in life is a bad attitude, and they won't even give you a handicapped parking license plate for that." The point is that what determines whether we feel bad or good, stuck or unstuck, is not so much determined by our negative or positive external circumstances as by our thoughts, beliefs, and attitude—our mindset.

Even though we may struggle to change our external circumstances, we really need to "get" that we are ultimately in charge of how we feel. It's possible to feel peaceful by praying, meditating, or going to church; by helping out another person; or by taking a long, brisk walk—even though our economic circumstances may not have changed. That is why the theme of this book is that stress begins in our mind, right between our ears.

Unfortunately, our mind frequently gets distracted, diverted, and sidetracked by the events going on around us. That is why it's imperative for you to take charge of your responses to stressors, especially your economic stressors, before they do you in.

And if you're seeking a healthier lifestyle, you're not alone. The president and the first family of America are setting a great example for the rest of us, modeling what health and vibrancy look like. When it comes to wellness, we're certainly a better nation for the example they offer America and the world.

Yet the ideas you'll find here actually go back thousands of years. More than 25 centuries ago, the Greek philosopher Plato perceived the truth of eternity when he saw that a sacred force, a supreme source of beauty, breathed human beings into life. He wrote that our soul's purpose was to ascend to that sacred force by glorifying nature and loving one another. You couldn't find a better Rx for stress relief than what I call the "Plato Prescription"—glorify nature and love one another. Just thinking about those ideas can relax us.

As we go forward together, you'll find that this book is as scientific as it is spiritual. I'm a Jewish doctor, and although I have Jewish roots, I have Christian wings and a Buddhist and Hindu outlook. Dr. Robert H. Schuller of the Crystal Cathedral invited me to present my preventive medicine and wellness philosophy as the Sunday speaker on the world-famous "The Hour of Power" TV show. I shared my vision of Integrative Medicine by first telling the audience that our health is too important to leave up to science, but also too important to be unscientific about. Then I shared my belief that God's presence is in every living thing, and that love is the greatest healer of all. When I was done, Dr. Schuller said to me on national television: "Dr. Taub, Jesus, like you, was a Jew...and both of you are on the very same wavelength."

Reader, please honor me with your trust. I've probably treated illnesses more than a million times since I began medical school 50 years ago, I've never refused to treat someone for lack of money, and my track record is among the best. So you have nothing to lose by trusting my intentions and my experience when I tell you that I can help you understand how to get back to shore!

Please join me on a scientific and spiritual journey to wholeness and peace of mind. You'll reap the rewards for the rest of your life!

CHAPTER 1

IT'S STILL AMERICA

I want a reason for the way things have to be
I need a hand to help build up some kind of hope inside of me...

And I'm...calling all angels
I'm calling all you angels

—LYRICS FROM "CALLING ALL ANGELS" BY THE MUSICAL GROUP TRAIN

If you watch the news, it's unquestionable that this is one of the most difficult times our nation has ever faced. The economy is in its worst shape perhaps since the Great Depression. We are fighting prolonged and difficult wars in Iraq and Afghanistan. Tens of millions of Americans have lost some or all of their investments and retirement funds. People are joking—although they aren't laughing about it—that their 401(k) has now become a 201(k). And when it comes to housing prices, it seems as if the nation is literally doing the limbo, wondering just how low prices can go.

We are bombarded with a constant drumbeat of negative statistics—job losses, plummeting earnings, collapsing banks, alarming rises in the cost of living, and foreclosures. If the numbers tell a story, the story is not a very happy one at all.

And even anecdotally, we hear from friends, relatives, and neighbors about layoffs, losses, and confusion over what is going to happen next. Bleak times, indeed.

Here is a list of key stressors affecting us today. When we think about the current economic situation, we see a host of money-related stressors:

- Loss of Job
- Loss of Income
- Loss of Home
- Loss of Retirement Income
- Loss of General Savings
- Loss of Confidence and Self-Esteem
- Loss of Dignity
- Totally Deflated Ego

When we seek news about what's happening in the economy, we get even more stressed because the news is often so bleak—job losses, industries in collapse, and even stress-related violence in our schools, homes, and workplaces.

Even in the best economic times, the following issues trigger stress...and they're exacerbated in times like these:

- Illness (yours or a friend's or loved one's)
- Obesity

- Overweight
- Drug and Alcohol Abuse
- Depression
- Divorce
- Children's Behavior
- Conflicts

And yet.

It's still America, the strongest, freest, most successful country in the history of the world. Never has one nation been able to offer sanctuary, hope, a fresh start, and an opportunity for success based on merit and hard work as has this nation. Never has one country stood so uniquely and powerfully as a beacon of inspiration and hope in a world of darkness.

I do not in any way wish to minimize the seriousness of the issues our nation—and our world—faces, and I certainly do not seek to minimize the pain that you, your loved ones, or those closest to you might be experiencing. But at the same time, it's essential for every American to know that while the bad news is trumpeted on every news station and on the front page of every newspaper and news magazine, the real news is that America is as resilient, strong, and creative as ever. The same qualities that built our nation into a shining city upon a hill are at work even as you read these words, creating a bright future for us as we put this temporary— and I emphasize the word temporary—period of negativity, doom, and gloom behind us.

Many successful business people will tell you that there is an astonishing amount of economic activity going on, even at the depths of what many call the worst recession since the Great Depression of the 1930s. People are starting, growing, and selling businesses. Jobs are being created. New products and services unimaginable even a few years ago, let alone a decade or a generation ago, continue to make the scene, and people are spending money on those things. Believe it or not, there are plenty of people who are making a great deal of money even in this economy. And they're doing it the old-fashioned way—by delivering outstanding products and services to the marketplace, and by working hard to keep their businesses strong.

But you don't hear about that on the news.

My purpose here is to counter the despair, the fear, the insecurity, and the outright terror that all too many Americans are experiencing in the light of this economic downturn and the way in which the media sometimes inflame those negative emotions. We create our realities first in our minds and then go out and find evidence to support the mental hypotheses we have constructed; then we live our lives in accordance with the world views we have adopted. This means that if we hear that things are bad, we will look for more evidence to support our belief that things are bad, and with that negative mentality, we are all but certain to create bad results for ourselves—in our health, in our careers, and in the lives of our families.

I'm going to show you how to use the awesome power of the amazing mind you possess so you can take your life in a direction of positivity, prosperity, and peace. I'm going to show you how to look at the world—how to look at *your* world—and cope, perhaps as never before, with the range of stressors, personal and financial, that face us all. I'll show you ways to radically reduce the level of unwanted, destructive stress in your life and provide you with a path toward personal recovery and wellness that you can follow even as our nation follows its own path to economic recovery.

I also want to remind you that your health, not your house or investment portfolio, is your most valuable asset. It's all too easy in times like these to neglect your health and to fail to do the "preventive maintenance" on our bodies that will keep you running strong. So we'll review the steps you can take, right now, regardless of what's happening on Wall Street or in Washington, D.C., to maximize your health and create the powerful mindset and attitude that will carry you through these admittedly challenging times.

This stress treatment works by freeing up life energy that is "stuck" inside you and generating even more life energy. This will in turn stimulate positive changes in your body and brain chemistry to help lift away despondency and despair. This approach makes you more available to take advantage of new beginnings and new opportunities, including jobs! For example, if you are stressed-out, you are obviously not as likely to find a new job or even leave the house to search for one. When you feel despondent, you're not as likely to get your résumé out there!

I advise my patients, when they're feeling especially down, to complete one project or reconcile one uncomfortable relationship. The energy thus created kick-starts momentum, and you'll eventually decide you can accomplish anything.

It's impossible for most of us, though, to turn a negative into a positive by using our own stressed-out thoughts. That's why you need to ask a Higher Power or your Guardian Angels for help—it's usually way too hard to help yourself when you are at the bottom of the stress hole.

There's a wonderful expression that dates back more than 1,500 years to the Jewish Talmud, an ancient source of spiritual wisdom: "I may not be able to change the world, but I can change myself." We cannot single-handedly transform the economy overnight. Nor can any one of us (unless we happen to be Rupert Murdoch) shift the way TV news or newspapers talk about what's going on in the economy. But we *can* make amazing, radical, and best of all, easy-to-adopt transformations in the way we respond to what's going on in the world.

We do not have to be the victims of an economic system that seems to have lost its course. While there are important structural changes that need to take place in the way our national global economy works, the good news is that those changes are being made. Too much is invested in freedom's future for our leaders to falter. But our own personal journeys to stress-free living and freedom from crippling anxiety and even depression do not require us to wait for the government, the business world, the banks, or anyone else to get their acts together. I'll show you how to find your own path toward emotional, physical, and spiritual freedom that is not linked in any way to the NASDAQ, to the unemployment rate, or to any other financial indicator. We're not just talking about the power of positive thinking, as important a component of this plan for living that it may be. Instead, I'm going to share with you an approach that you could call the power of positive living that offers a life of joy, happiness, and fulfillment that many of us are far too stressed-out even to imagine.

And stress is the number one offender.

Stress erodes our health. It destroys our confidence. It chokes off our ability to love others, because we can become so consumed with worry that we do not give or receive love from those who matter most to us. Stress can land us in the hospital, in divorce court, even in the grave. I'm writing because the glum economic news has triggered an epidemic of stress that is reaching out and harming the lives of virtually every man, woman, and child in our nation. As a physician and healer, I simply cannot stand by and allow this epidemic to go unchecked. Can a single book change the world? Well, if you're going to come with me on this journey, it can transform your life. And to return to the Talmud, its authors wrote that if a person saves one life, it is as if he has saved the entire world. My goal is to change *your* world.

One theme of American mythology is that of the frontiersman who goes it alone, the John Wayne type.

Those old John Wayne movies are terrific; unfortunately, they give a startlingly incorrect impression about how people succeed. As with practically anything important, we don't succeed entirely through our own efforts. Let me illustrate with this famous story from World War II about an individual who approached a fighter pilot in a restaurant after the war:

"Excuse me, I don't mean to interrupt your meal," the stranger said. "But didn't you fly more than a hundred missions off an aircraft carrier in the Pacific?"

The fighter pilot, surprised and pleased to be recognized for his accomplishments, asked the stranger how he knew all that about him.

"I packed your parachute," the stranger replied.

Whether we are flying combat missions or simply getting through the day-to-day issues and challenges of domestic life, we are more likely to succeed if we don't try to go it alone. Unfortunately, one of the reactions that most people have to stress is to isolate, to fail to seek help, and to "John Wayne" it. I'd like to share with you a different way.

Almost 40 years ago, in 1972, a Senator named Tom Eagleton was offered the vice presidential role on the Democratic ticket. But before the ink was barely dry on the bumper stickers, it was revealed that Senator Eagleton had received treatment for mental health issues. The nation was aghast that someone who had admitted he needed a boost in terms of his mental health could be "a heartbeat from the presidency," and Senator Eagleton was quickly and unceremoniously dropped from the vice presidential candidacy.

How times have changed.

Or have they?

Remarkably, for all the inroads that mental health awareness has made in our society, many of us are still resistant to the idea of seeking help for our problems. Instead, we follow the John Wayne path, sticking to our old ideas of how life should be instead of recognizing the truth about how it is and determining how best we can improve it with the use of new ideas.

The greatest golfer in the world, Tiger Woods, has a swing coach, an individual whose full-time job is simply to work with Tiger on his swing and to help Woods challenge Jack Nicklaus for the title of greatest golfer in history. Admittedly, golf is a complicated game. But if it's OK for the greatest golfer of his era to seek help for the game of golf, why isn't it acceptable for us as individuals to seek help with the infinitely more complex game of life that we must play every day?

Fortunately, an enormous amount of help is available. In these pages, you'll find the distilled essence of what we in the healing profession know about counteracting and reducing stress. And you'll find all kinds of practical, sensible, down-to-earth, easy-to-apply ideas about eliminating the negative effects of stress from your life.

And yet, there's another kind of help of which we can avail ourselves, and in this case, I am speaking of spiritual help.

My greatest disagreement with the way Western medicine is taught and practiced has to do with the fact that science and spirituality have been so divided in our society that they appear to be on opposite sides of the Grand Canyon. On the South Rim, where most people visit, you'll find all the tests, the equipment, the computer, and the medications. On the North Rim, the seemingly less accessible side, is the realm of the spirit and the role of the spirit in healing. I wouldn't want to pave over the Grand Canyon, but I would like to close the gap in our thinking that separates the scientific from the spiritual. All of the practical ideas I'll share with you about stress management can only go so far.

At its root, I see stress as a spiritual illness, and a spiritual problem requires a spiritual solution. I'm not necessarily talking about organized religion—I'm not going to tell you to pray in a certain way, at a certain time, or using certain specified language. Some people love and are comforted by the religion with which they grew up. Others are turned off by it. Whether you follow the religious path of your early years or not, I don't mean spirituality in some vague, confusing sense. I simply mean that one of the most powerful ways to eliminate the toxicity of stress is by reconnecting with your spirit, which tends to get buried, especially in times like these, under a mountain of anxiety, depression, and fear. We're going to cast all those negative emotions aside and reconnect with that part of us that reflects and connects us to our Higher Power.

Cardiologists Meyer Friedman and Ray H. Rosenman, who created the term "Type A behavior" to define the constellation of aggressive traits that leads to heart attacks and other fatal illnesses, wrote: "Never before in human history have so many people sought to live in so deep a spiritual void."

What's amazing about their observation is that they were writing not in the year 2009 or 1995. Indeed, they wrote those words all the way back in 1964. So stress has always been with us, although it's fair to say that it may never have been as prevalent and damaging as it is today.

So as we ask for help and new ideas, and as we seek to incorporate the benefits of a spiritual approach to life (which we'll discuss in detail throughout this book), it's time for us to do what wise individuals have always done when the going got rough: call for the help of angels to bring us to a healthier, happier, more successful way of life.

One of our greatest presidents, Abraham Lincoln, had no qualms about asking Americans to seek their "better angels" as civil war descended on our great nation. I believe that *we* should be calling on angels if we are to live happily and successfully. Therefore, in each chapter, I will introduce you to the Guardian Angel whose spirit most exemplifies the topic that we are discussing, and I'll offer you ways in which to bring the blessings of that angel into your life.

There really are at least two ways to call on angels. One is to reach out for help, simply through the act of talking or listening to your angels. And the second is through action.

Action activates angels! In each chapter, you'll meet a different angel to help you manage the burden of stress in your life. And you'll find the specific actions to take to find that angel at your side as you cope with the events of your day.

In this first chapter, since we're calling all angels, let's call on the Angel of Hope. I love the concept of hope, because I find it invigorating and life-sustaining. Hope by its very nature implies that we see before us the possibility of a better day, restored health, better relationships, increased financial success, or growth in any area of our lives. Join with me now in inviting the Guardian Angel of Hope into your life. You wouldn't be reading a book about stress if you weren't experiencing a fair amount right now. There's hope and there's help, and you don't have to go on hurting the way you've been hurting.

In the Bible, the word for healing is related to the verb "to loosen," as if a doctor is loosening a patient from the bonds of illness. It's my goal to deliver these ancient healing powers to your life, to loosen you from a mental picture of the world that is causing you to stress, and to bring warmth, light, and joy into your life as never before. With the Angel of Hope at our side, and as we call on all the angels whose unique properties can transform us, we are sure to succeed.

This book exists because of my own profound commitment to healing, to loosening the bonds of illness, and to bringing warmth to those I serve, whether in my medical practice or in the broader wellness-oriented community. It's time to recognize that it's still America. Regardless of what is going on in the economy or in your personal situation, things can and will improve for you. Belief in a stronger, healthier, more vibrant tomorrow is the essence of the American way. So let's remember who we are as we go forward together on a journey to wellness like no other.

*

TO CALL ON THE GUARDIAN ANGEL OF HOPE...

Tune out the news. Stop watching, listening, or reading about the financial, political, and war news. Paying attention to these things frazzles our nerves and creates in us a sense of hopelessness. When we tune out the bad news in the outer world, we have a chance to experience peace in our own inner world. This is where the healing begins. This is the first critical step you can take on the path to ridding your life of unhealthy stress.

CHAPTER 2

WHAT IS STRESS, ANYWAY?

If you're out of work, it's a recession. If I'm out of work,
it's a depression.

—ANONYMOUS

What is stress, anyway? Let's begin by defining our terms. For our purposes, stress is a destructive reaction to a situation we perceive as negative or even dangerous. What sorts of things trigger a stress reaction? Bad economic news on TV. Notice of a late payment. Raised voices at home. Rush-hour traffic. An e-mail from a boss, coworker, or client. You name it. The important thing to recognize is that stress isn't what's happening in the world around us or even in our personal lives. Stress is our response or reaction to those events or pieces of information. This distinction is extremely important, because we can seldom control the actions of other people, whether we're talking about our spouse, our grown children, or even the President of the United States. What we can control, however, is our own personal "strategy" for reacting to stressful events.

There's a scene in the movie *Singing in the Rain* when the head of the studio informs the character Cosmo, played by Donald O'Connor, that the studio is shutting down in order to change from silent movies to sound films. Cosmo, suddenly out of work, grins and says, "At last I can start suffering and write that symphony!" To which the studio head responds that he's putting Cosmo in as head of the new Music Department.

Cosmo grins again. "Well, thanks, R.F.! At last I can *stop* suffering and write that symphony."

What's funny about that scene is that in the first exchange, Cosmo thinks he's been fired. And yet instead of getting stressed out about what he's going to do for money, how he's going to pay his rent, or thinking about how his mother told him he would never amount to anything, he turns it into a positive—now he has time to do the serious composing that he could never manage while he was still working as a pianist at the movie studio.

And then the situation shifts a moment later when it turns out that Cosmo has been given even more responsibilities than ever, as the head of the Music Department for the entire studio. Cosmo's response isn't to start freaking out about all his new responsibilities, whether he'll succeed in the new job, or anything negative like that. Instead, he essentially responds, just as eagerly, that with the certainty of a higher income, he'll be able to do the serious composing that he's always wanted to do.

Okay, that's the movies. In real life, when people think they have lost their job, they don't start smiling and talking about composing a symphony. Or if, as is often the case today, they find that their work responsibilities have been radically increased, they don't smile and start talking about creative projects they'll be doing on the side.

Speaking of work and jobs, it's interesting that in the Bible, Job was the name of the guy who needed to test his love for God; Job's job was to love God—whenever he didn't, he got really stressed.

Comedy is the art of the unexpected, and the expected course for those of us who lose our jobs or have more to do is to get stressed out. So the question is this: How can we move from a mentality that translates every change in our lives into a stressful threat and move to a thought pattern that embraces or at least accepts change?

By the way, not all stress is negative! The noted scientist Hans Selye, who dramatically demonstrated the existence of biological stress, offered a distinction between distress, or negative stress, which afflicts so many of us, and eu-stress, or positive stress. Is there such a thing as positive stress? If you've ever enjoyed watching or competing in a close athletic contest, card or board games, or a great horse race, or battling a work deadline on a project you enjoy, I think you'll agree with me that not all stress is harmful.

My key point here is that stress is not what happens out there. It's what happens in here—*between our ears.* It's what happens in our own minds and thinking patterns when a stressful situation suddenly arises.

For most of us, the stress response is best described as the instinctual, self-protecting thought pattern called "flight or fight." Someone or something *challenges* us—another driver on the road. A teenage child. An angry boss. An irate customer. A precipitous drop in the Dow Jones average. Your 401(k) plan in tatters. Or heaven forbid, a foreclosure notice.

Our first instinct may be to fight back—to express our displeasure at the other person in verbal or nonverbal means. Or sometimes we just want to take a swing at somebody. Rarely does this kind of activity make things better.

The opposite side of the spectrum is flight. Conflict arises, and we want to run away. We might escape physically, by leaving a stress-filled workplace or marriage. We might drop out of school or a relationship if we find the expectations too stressful. Or we might escape to some sort of addictive behavior that soothes the upset feelings.

What's good about the fight-or-flight reaction to stress is that if you only encounter one stressful situation a week, you're in great shape. The stressful event occurs, your body's internal chemistry set floods your bloodstream with adrenaline and other appropriate chemicals, you handle the threat, and you go on with your life. That's how things worked for our cave-dwelling ancestors tens of thousands of years ago. The problem is that in modern life, we are bombarded with stressors on a minute-by-minute basis. Try these on for size:

Your boss is yelling at you, your most important client is calling you on your cell phone, and there are a hundred and one (and counting!) e-mails in your inbox.

While you're at home trying to get the laundry done and take care of the house, your five-year-old, home sick from school, starts demanding your attention so loudly that he wakes the baby.

And we haven't even talked about what's on the dining-room table—that stack of unpaid bills, or the statement showing the plummeting value of your 401(k), or a notice about your mortgage or rent being overdue.

Our bodies were meant to handle only a limited number of stressful situations. And yet modern life is an infinite source of stressors, from the moment the alarm clock jars us out of a peaceful sleep until we lay our weary heads on the pillow after another long and often frustrating day. They give medals to military heroes, but when you think about it, just getting on with the act of living, of working, of raising a family, is also heroic. Where are the medals for Mother of the Year? Or Employee of the Week? Or Grandparents Who Care? We should all be getting those awards every day. But we don't. Instead, we find ourselves awakening each day, like in the movie *Groundhog Day*, to a series of challenges and stresses that threaten to overwhelm us emotionally, physically, and spiritually.

So when we talk about stress, we're not talking only about the individual stressful moments that we face in the best way we can, sometimes with dignity and sometimes without. We're also talking about the cumulative effects of stressor piled on stressor, until we have literally stressed our bodies out, running our systems on adrenaline, norepinephrine, caffeine, sugar, alcohol, and other stimulants in an effort to find the energy to face modern life on life's terms.

Let's put it another way. A NASCAR racecar is built to handle the stress of a road race lasting, say, 500 miles. The designers of a racecar create the car to exceed the stresses that will be placed on it—heat, competition, the grade and length of the specific track on which it will be racing, and similar factors.

Now take that same magnificently constructed NASCAR vehicle...and use it as a taxi on the streets of New York City.

About how long do you think it's going to last?

To put it simply, our bodies were created for one set of stresses, but because of the incessant demands of technology and modern life, we are overtaxing them on a day-by-day and minute-by-minute basis. The same racecar that can win at Daytona would be smoking rubble after just 24 hours on the streets of Manhattan.

So how do we get the vehicles with which we travel through life—our body, our minds, our spirits—"in tune" with the relentless demands that modern life presents?

It isn't easy, but it is doable.

It all starts with the recognition that we have the power to shift the way we respond to stressful news. Much like the story from *Singing in the Rain*, we have choices about how we cope with seeming adversity, or if you read the pages of today's newspapers, complete catastrophe.

I mentioned in the previous chapter that we would be calling all angels to come to our aid as we transform ourselves on this journey to stress-free living. In this chapter, let s call upon the Guardian Angel of Peace.

If there were ever a time for the Angel of Peace to descend into the world and calm things down, it's right now! Our world is anything but peaceful. Sad to say, the wars in Iraq and Afghanistan are only two of the violent conflicts that are occurring across the planet at any given time. Layer in the war that the leaders of radical Islam are fomenting against much of Western society, and the subsequent War on Terror of our own, and the whole world feels like a battleground. It's no wonder that our individual spirits may feel battle-weary. It's hard to live life to the fullest when we think about all the suffering and depravity in the world around us.

Angel of Peace, come on down! And even if we could somehow wave a magic wand and make war disappear, and I'd like to believe we could if enough people so desired, we're still left with a world of technology and the increasing stress that all our technological achievements have created.

We move at technology's speed—not the other way around. Consider transportation. In the nineteenth century, scientists "proved" that human beings could never travel at more than 40 miles an hour, so there was no sense in building trains that went that fast. The human body simply couldn't take it. And as for flying—well, that was something for the science fiction writers. Fast forward, with the emphasis on the word *fast,* to the current day. We can go a lot faster than 40 miles an hour. Or can we? Think of all the stress that accumulates from being stuck in traffic or stuck on the tarmac waiting for your flight to take off. And even if there is no traffic and we could travel as fast as we would like, the mere fact that we have such incredible transportation marvels at our service means that we create astonishingly hectic lifestyles for ourselves. Whether we are business people or homemakers, we expect to cover as much ground in a week as our great-grandparents might have covered in their entire lives.

Or take the speed of information. Even a generation ago, if you wanted to get information about something, *you wrote a letter.* You would send off a letter, and it would take a few days for the letter to get there. It would then take the recipient a few days to respond to your request, and your answer would come by return mail a few days after that. Then came faxes, and guaranteed overnight delivery, and e-mail, and instant messaging, and MySpace and Facebook and Twitter...you get the point. Today, information travels so quickly that if someone fails to respond to an e-mail, instant message, or a comment on their Facebook page within minutes, we start to go crazy.

And we haven't even begun to scratch the surface of stress in the workplace or in our schools. Our societal mindset of scarcity has created competition instead of collaboration as the dominant means of doing things. The good news about technology is that the Internet is making for a more collaborative world…for some. For most people, competition from coworkers, from other businesses, and even from labor pools and other countries creates a stressed-out world of anxiety and fear.

It just isn't possible for most of us to turn the clock back to a more bucolic time when we were governed by nature's rhythms, a time when we worked on our farms during the day and viewed with awe a canopy of stars over our heads at night. Instead, we live in a world of incessant demands, and for so many of us, it feels as if there just simply isn't enough time (let alone money) to get to everything on our agendas.

If we were to examine any given day in our lives and ask what percentage of the activities in which we engage are stressful and which are soothing, the ratio might be something like 50 to 1. There's probably not a single person on the planet, therefore, who couldn't do with a little more peace in his or her life.

So the message of the Angel of Peace is this: There will always be sources of stress in our lives. The question is how to respond to those sources. We can be like our cave-person ancestors and engage in a now endless process of fight or flight. Or we can be like Cosmo and *manage our reactions to stressors* so that our lives are peaceful instead of filled with conflict and fear.

The great motivator Earl Nightingale would tell the story of two sons of an alcoholic father. One became an alcoholic and ruined his life.

"With a father like that, what else could I do?"

The other son abstained from drinking, worked hard at securing an education, and went out and became very successful in the world.

"With a father like that," he reasoned, "what else could I do?"

In other words, stress isn't about what happens *out there,* whether the "out there" to which we are referring is the gloomy economic situation or even an unhappy spouse. Stress begins and ends inside of us. The Angel of Peace guides us to recognize that stressors—things that can trigger stress—don't always create the same results in different people, just like Nightingale's example of the two sons. Stress isn't what happens. Stress is something we create through our reaction to what happens.

The good news is that we have choices about how we are going to respond to the many stresses of modern life. And the most important place where we need to practice the art of stress-free living…is in our own homes. And that's the subject of our next chapter.

*

TO CALL ON THE GUARDIAN ANGEL OF PEACE...

Recognize that even if you are feeling uncomfortable and downtrodden by events that seem beyond your control, you have the power to restore peace in your mind by learning healthy ways to cope with the realities of your daily life.

Believe that if you take one genuine step toward God, that God will take a hundred steps toward you; if you cry one genuine tear, then God will wipe away a thousand.

Invite the Angel of Peace to help you respond to the stressors in your life with choices that can put you on a path that leads away from discomfort and toward acceptance and joy.

CHAPTER 3

RECONNECTING WITH OUR FAMILIES

Home is the place where, when you have to go there,
they have to take you in.

—ROBERT FROST

A generation ago, a New York television station began its evening news with a deep-voice asking, in an ominous tone, "It's 10:00 P.M. Do you know where your children are?"

Parents today could be asked the same question at 5:00 P.M., at midnight, and at 2:00 A.M., for that matter. Thanks to great technological advances, and the necessity in most families for both spouses to work, the family unit is under siege perhaps more than ever before. And at a time when parents are worried about keeping their jobs and when high school and college-age students are worried about ever finding one, the stresses on families have never been greater.

Empty nesters and retirees are feeling the pain, too. Many people who have disciplined themselves throughout their lives to save money have seen as much as 40 percent of their savings vanish almost overnight. Even conservative investors who sought to make just 5 percent on their money are now earning just 2 percent. Older Americans were brought up on the magic of compound interest…but the interest on zero savings is zero! Yikes!

The home is supposed to be a sanctuary, a place where family members find connection with each other and respite from the pressures of a crazy world. Today, those pressures have found their way inside the front door of the family to a greater degree than ever before. Technology is the most obvious culprit, but it is hardly the only offender. Let's take a look at the ways in which the home has become a source of stress instead of a source of love and satisfaction.

Too much month at the end of the money.

Unfortunately, the troubled economy translates into trouble at home. Americans are worried about how they are going to keep their homes if they lose their jobs. Many older Americans are worried about how they will survive now that much of their savings has been wiped out. For the first time in recent economic history, even some families where the parents are educated and hardworking are finding themselves unable to find work, on the verge of homelessness, and needing to request government or private charitable assistance. More and more families are on the verge of dropping out of the middle class and into poverty and deprivation. This is what makes today's situation unlike any other since the Great Depression.

More screens than ever.

Even if the economy were doing just fine, there are still plenty of new challenges that confront today's American family. For example, Mom, Dad, Billy, and Sue might all be under the same roof, but they might as well be on different planets. That's because each may be glued to his or her own TV screen. Mom may be in her home office checking e-mail; Dad is watching a game. Sue may be on Facebook with her friends, some of whom she knows and some of whom she doesn't. And who knows what Billy may be doing on the computer behind his locked bedroom door! All the ads say that the Internet fosters community. What kind of community can you really have when everyone in the same home is staring at a different screen?

Along those lines, have you ever noticed that in ads selling everything from health care to financial services, family members are gazing contentedly...but not at each other. That's right—they're looking at computer screens. A father and small son stare happily at a laptop where, we are told, they are reviewing their wonderful health plan. A couple in their sixties is glowing with delight as they study their retirement funds on a computer screen. (Oops—that image must be more than a year old!) Even in business meetings portrayed in advertisements, people often are not looking at each other. Instead, they're staring at those darned screens. The problem is that when you're screening information, you're screening your loved ones out.

Turning youth into a commodity.

A couple of decades ago, some smart marketer figured out that preteens and teenagers lead the nation in disposable income and have not yet made their possibly lifelong choices for the brands of shampoo, deodorant, soda, and other products they will consume. So marketers created an entire youth culture, complete with TV networks that specialize in appealing only to younger viewers. The basic theme of many of those programs and the advertisements on those shows is that adults—especially your parents—are too old and stupid to be useful guides about how to spend your money. And the more you spend to differentiate yourself from them, the happier you will be.

As a result, our families are now cultural battlegrounds with a war going on between the things that Mom and Dad enjoy and the things that marketers are hoping to sell to preteens and teenagers. The youth culture, which displays itself in fashion, music, literature, and other forms of entertainment, has driven a wedge between parents and children. We see that Hollywood is raising America's youth, often with undesirable results.

The rise—and fall—of two-worker families.

For several decades now, it has become more and more difficult for a sole breadwinner to support a family. Part of this is due to the increasing tax burden in our society, and part is due to the ever-increasing appetite for consumer and luxury goods. While every woman who wishes to work should have the freedom to succeed in her career, and while she is entitled to equal pay for equal work, we are now living in a world where many women who wish they had the choice to stay home with their children simply cannot afford to do so.

The inevitable stresses and strains of the two-worker family take their toll on life in the home. Is Mom expected to shop, clean, and cook in addition to working a full-time job? Does Dad have the right to go out and play a round of golf on Saturday morning if his wife is exhausted from working two jobs—one inside the home and one outside? And what happens in today's economy, when one parent is out of work and the other parent now bears the full financial responsibility for the home? All of these issues raise the stress level in today's marriages.

The advent of the throwaway marriage.

It used to be that couples married with an expectation that they would stay married for the rest of their lives. As divorces become more prevalent in our society, that expectation seems to be diminishing. Some young people may marry today with a jaundiced eye, aware as they are of the staggering divorce rates and pragmatic enough not to expect with absolute certainty that their own marriage will be the one to beat the odds.

When the anti-divorce ethic was at its strongest in our society, until just a few decades ago, there were indeed more people locked into loveless marriages. So it's a benefit to those whose relations really do not work that they can cut their losses and start over with someone else. On the other hand, the downside of the widespread acceptance and de-stigmatizing of divorce in our society may cause couples to think that it is acceptable to throw in the towel without making a strong enough stand for their marriages. The resulting trend of divorces increases the percentage of children from separated families and increases the likelihood that those children will view marriage as a temporary state.

So what's a family to do? There have been a million books written about being married and raising children, but no one has yet written "The Manual"—the ultimate guide to handling all questions as they arise. The challenges of marriage and family are thus multiplied in a moment in time like ours, when economic news is grim and the solutions risky and unproven.

It's truly time to call upon our third angel, the Guardian Angel of Love, to work its magic in our beleaguered, economically challenged, and overly technological homes. In the Bible, we learn that love does not envy. In today's world, we need to realize that love does not e-mail. It doesn't text, Twitter, or go on Facebook. Instead, real love turns on when the technology is turned off. Every family needs a technology-free zone in the house, a place where family members can disconnect from the Internet, from their iPhones, and from their BlackBerrys and reconnect with their loved ones.

The Angel of Love does not require Wi-Fi, or wireless Internet technology, to be reached. If anything, this angel flies as fast and as far as she can from anything to do with technology. To manage the level of stress in our homes, we need to detach from the computer screens and reattach with our spouses, our children, and our parents. The problem is that human beings crave variety, and technology offers just that. Who's going to send the next text message? Who's going to fire off an e-mail to you? Who's on your Facebook? The only way to find out is to plug in. And yet, all that disconnection, one family member from the other, is a major source of stress within many families today.

In the sixties, psychologist Timothy Leary, who formed an LSD advocacy group, told his followers to "turn on, tune in, and drop out." Our mission today is radically different. The Angel of Love wants us instead to turn off our technological devices, tune in to each other's spirits, and reconnect. Otherwise, there is no room for this angel to work her magic.

Is your TV on during the dinner hour? It needs to be turned off. TV advertisers are blatant about their desire to make members of the family look up from the dinner table. The TV, in other words, is actively engaged in trying to interrupt your conversation. Not only that, the ratings for news broadcasts skyrocket when the nation is gripped with fear, whether it's about an epidemic of bad economic news or a swine flu pandemic. So your TV wants to scare you.

Now you might be asking, "What family dinner are you talking about? Our family hasn't eaten together since the Carter administration."

Would it be possible for your family to set aside specific times for family meals? It may take a little bit of effort, but it is possible to align the schedules of family members to create a single dinner hour. I acknowledge that this may be an uncomfortable option at first. But when a family dines together on a regular basis and truly has the opportunity for conversation uninterrupted by a cell phone that must be answered or a wide-screen TV that refuses to be ignored, the benefits are enormous.

This applies just as much to empty nesters and retirees as it does to those engaged in the challenge of raising children. If anything, a couple's need for communication and face-to-face time only increases when the children have moved on to college or other coming-of-age activities. And as for couples who don't have children, it's all too easy to allow for technology to become the modern version of the newspaper sections behind which married people hide. Lovers of the world, unite! You have nothing to lose but a half hour of TV news.

Nowadays, practically all forms of communication, photos, and video can be reduced to the "zeros and ones" code transmitted wirelessly into our homes. Love, however, cannot be reduced to a digital transmission. There is a power that comes from individuals sitting in a room together, looking into each other's eyes, and telling each other about what's on his or her mind.

How do we thaw cold or even frozen relationships within families? By sitting down at the dinner table, by looking each other in the eye, and by screening out all the screens that have come to dominate our lives.

We live in a time of unparalleled individual freedom, which is great, because now people can live, work, marry, and raise children pretty much as they choose. The problem is that as a society, we may have swung a little too far in the direction of individualism. We aren't thinking enough about the fact that the building block of any successful society, from ancient times to our day, is the family. Stress and loneliness are often bound up one with the other. Certainly some choose to live alone, and they cannot be faulted for that choice. But studies show that the happiest people, and those with the longest life span, have families and marriages that are healthy, vibrant, and strong.

Of course, I don't mean to minimize the effects of some of the truly devastating social ills that, unfortunately, have been visited on families, such as addiction, mental illness, emotional and even sexual abuse.

The good news is that our culture now supports family healing from these issues whereas in the past, such matters might have been swept under the carpet, something too embarrassing for the neighbors to know about. Today, our neighbors may be just as messed up as we are. So the good news is that there is no longer anything to hide. In every family system where love is not freely given and received, it takes one courageous individual to step up and say, "It's time for a change. We need help. Who's with me?"

If you are that individual, take heart. Help is available in so many forms today, often at little or no cost. There's no shame in a family having a problem; the only shame is if that family does not seek to solve that problem.

Even in families where love exists and the TV and the Internet do not dominate the social discourse, it's still possible for family members to feel unloved. It's our responsibility as parents and spouses always to remind our loved ones that we do love them and never to assume that "They know I love them." There are some messages that cannot be delivered often enough.

As our lives grow increasingly complicated, as much of our economy continues to sputter, as we bring the gift of children into our home, as our work lives become more intense, and as the pace of life itself seems to move at warp speed, the first casualty is often intimacy between husband and wife. If this is happening in your marriage, you are not alone. But if this happening, you are at considerable risk of loss of love unless you and your partner literally schedule time, ideally on a nightly basis, to just sit together and discuss the events of the day. But make sure that you're talking about *your* day, not whatever fear-mongering that took place on the news that day.

These intimacy sessions, even if brief due to the exhaustion of both parties, can often make the difference between a successful marriage and one that fails. These sessions need not be about problem solving or troubleshooting within the home. They can just be a chance to talk about…whatever, the same way you did when you and your beloved were just getting to know each other and you could talk for hours. (Remember those times? Ever wonder why you had so much to say back then and so little now?)

We can compare a love relationship to a bank account. When we meet someone, we give that person a certain amount of credits in the account, just because that person seems nice. Every time we have a positive interaction, more credits are deposited in the bank. When a high enough level of credits is established, we say to ourselves, "I love that person!" And when an even higher level is reached, we may propose marriage.

The problem with marriage is that it creates all too many opportunities for withdrawals from that account. When we live with another person, we see them not just at their best but at their worst, and on a daily basis. Having those moments of intimacy in the evening can create an opportunity for a couple to restore lost credits and make new deposits. The result: a marriage that works.

Most people think that stress comes when we don't have enough time for our loved ones. In reality, we all have 24 hours a day to spend. The trouble comes when we fail to *make* time for the ones we love.

So start making time tonight. Let the Angel of Love work her magic on your home, and watch the stress melt away.

*

TO CALL ON THE GUARDIAN ANGEL OF LOVE...

Turn off your technology, create a daily (or several-times-a-week) family dinner hour, look your loved ones in the eye, tell them you love them, and create a time of quiet intimacy for yourself and your spouse or partner each night before you retire. And always remember, love is all there is.

CHAPTER 4

GOOD NEWS: YOU HAVE MORE CONTROL THAN YOU THINK

If you feel like you've got everything under control,
you aren't going fast enough.

—RACING LEGEND MARIO ANDRETTI

Stress is generated by an overwhelming sense that we can't control our personal world—that we've run out of options. The good news is that there are vital ways in which you can manage stress in your life, regardless of what your boss, co-workers, spouse, children, relatives, or friends said or did... or, for that matter, how the value of your investments or pension changed in the last 24 hours! In this chapter, we're going to explore many ways in which you can manage the impact of stress in your life.

Let's go back to the example of NASCAR. Usually, after a race, sportswriters interview the driver who came in first. But now let's do an imaginary interview with the driver who came in last.

"What happened out there?" the reporter asks.

"You could say we had a bad day on the track," the driver admits.

"How come?"

"Well, we never really changed the oil. We ran on four bald tires for most of the race. I didn't get a good night's sleep last night, so I was pretty tired as I was driving. Some of the other teams have millions of dollars to spend to make their cars perfect. We haven't got that kind of money. So a lot of the parts in my car were failing and hadn't been replaced since the last race. The radio didn't work very well, so communication with my pit crew was spotty. And my attitude was pretty poor. Frankly, I didn't care whether we won or lost."

"I guess it's no wonder that you came in last."

"I guess you're right," the driver agrees. "I just figured that I didn't have a chance out there, so I kind of quit before I started. I just felt so out of control."

Now, no self-respecting NASCAR driver gets behind the wheel with that kind of attitude, unprepared mentally or physically. And yet, we all sometimes feel out of control in our own lives, especially when the Dow is down, unemployment is up, and the world economy seems to be going sideways.

Whether we're talking about a NASCAR "Car of Tomorrow" or your family minivan, if we don't take care of that vehicle, it's just not going to run in an optimal way. The same thing is true of ourselves. And yet, we're more likely to take better care of our cars than we do of ourselves.

Have you ever noticed that the same piece of information, whether it's personal, business, or financial, can cause a great deal of emotional distress at night, but if you hear the same thing after a good night's sleep, you can handle it much better? It's true. Whatever's going on in our lives, we can handle it better if we aren't exhausted and frustrated from everything else that's going on in our lives. (That's why a lot of smart people never check their e-mail at night.)

In previous chapters, we've talked about some ways of reducing the effect of external stress in our lives—detaching from technology, spending a little more quality time with our loved ones, things like that. In this chapter, we're going to talk about the things that we can do in our own lives that reduce the effect of those external stressors. It's really about keeping our "vehicle" in tiptop shape as we go around the track that is our lives.

To look at it from another angle, people generally feel happy when they have a sense that they can exert some control over their lives. Human beings relish the feeling of "being in charge." We like to keep our homes and workplaces a certain way. We like to do things in the order that makes most sense to us. We like to have that sense of control, especially when the world is filled with turmoil (which is how things look if you pay too much attention to the news).

Conversely, when we feel out of control, when we feel that events or other people are controlling our lives, we tend to be miserable. That's how many people feel today, given the challenging economic times in which we find ourselves.

Nobody likes to be bossed around, and that's just as true of a 5-year-old on a playground as it is of a 45-year-old at the office or a 75-year old in a retirement community. Our current economic situation has given millions and millions of Americans a highly uncomfortable feeling that they are not in control of their lives and fortunes. For many, that sense of loss of control is just as painful as the loss of money they experienced in their retirement accounts or even the loss of their jobs.

So the question becomes this: How is it possible for people to increase the amount of control they have over their lives, especially in this time of economic meltdown?

I put the words "good news" deliberately into the title of this chapter, because I want you to know that there are many ways in which you can increase the sense of control you feel, regardless of what is going on. And in order to assist us in making these changes, we're going to call on the Guardian Angel of Strength.

We do have enormous strength to dictate the course of our lives, regardless of external forces like the economy, the threat of terrorism, or war, the main external realities in our world today. And the wonderful news about the power we possess is that by making healthier choices about our lives, by grasping the levers of power in our day-to-day existence, we make ourselves stronger, more resilient, happier, and less prone to the negative effects of stress. So with the help of the Angel of Strength, who is standing by to give us the love, guidance, and assistance we need, let's take a look at some surprisingly simple—and surprisingly effective—things we can do right now in order to increase our sense of personal strength, make ourselves healthier, happier, and stronger, and knock stress out of the box.

Take a hike.

For some Americans, the thought of exercise is so upsetting that they want to lie down until it passes! We Americans have bulked up, but not at the gym like Arnold Schwarzenegger. As restaurant portions have gotten larger and "corporate food"—food manufactured without regard for your health—has gotten tastier, the average American has put on 10 to 15 pounds more than he or she was carrying a decade or so ago.

An unfit body often does not have the resilience necessary to handle the stresses and strains of everyday life, let alone a period of challenge and upset such as we are experiencing today. This means that getting off the couch has become—literally—a matter of life or death.

The human body was born to move. Our ancestors did not sit in cubicles for 8 to 10 hours a day, hunched over a computer screen. They were running, chasing, farming, hunting, playing, and dancing—all the things that we have somehow left behind. If a visitor from another planet were to come to Earth and study our lives, he might conclude that our sole purpose (our soul purpose???) as human beings is to stare at computer screens!

The good news is that you don't have to do anything radical to get in shape. Studies have shown that taking a brisk walk has the same cardiovascular benefits for you as going for a run. Many people belong to health clubs and gyms but don't go. You can dust off your membership card and grab a group exercise class or hire a trainer to take you around, give you a healthy routine to follow, and get started…or just start walking! Recent studies indicate that weight training is especially important for older folks seeking to maintain healthy bones and muscles. The word exercise is so unpleasant for some people that I prefer the word "movement." Dancing counts. Walking counts. So do gardening, doing housework, and playing with your grandchildren.

The key to success in establishing a new exercise—I mean, movement—program is to set low quotas for yourself. We know a man who says that when he goes to the gym, all he has to do is a few sit-ups and then he can go home. Of course, since he's gone to all the trouble of putting on his workout clothes and making it all the way there, once he does a few sit-ups, he's hardly likely to leave. You can trick yourself into optimal health like our friend. You can also call on the Angel of Strength to get you off the couch and moving.

The traditional guidance that fitness professionals offer is to take 10,000 steps a day, which sounds like a lot, but it can basically be accomplished in 30 to 60 minutes of fairly brisk walking. You don't have to walk 10,000 steps the first day. Just take a few more steps today than you did yesterday and a few more steps tomorrow. You'll look better, feel better, and most important for our purposes, get healthier. Exercise increases your immunity to stress, and after a while, you'll find that the things that used to bother you enormously today (not to mention those extra unwanted pounds) will just slide away.

Incidentally, moderate sunshine is essential for good health. Our parents were right when they told us to go outside and play. Vitamin D is best absorbed from natural sunlight, so unless it's blazingly hot and sunny where you are, it's important to get out and be in the sun for at least 20 minutes a day if you can manage it.

Fitness counts...so take a hike. Or do one push-up. Or one sit-up. (And see if you don't find yourself doing more.) If it's not possible to get outdoors, do yourself a favor and take a vitamin D supplement.

Do the right thing.

As Mark Twain said, "If I don't tell any lies, I don't have to remember anything." Admittedly, we live in a world where it sometimes seems as if morality has been stood upside down. The subprime loan mess. AIG. Bernie Madoff's Ponzi scheme. Today, it seems that the very same bankers who played a role in damaging the Economy are receiving government-approved multimillion-dollar bonuses and bailouts. We ask if it is fair that our tax dollars are being used to revive the institutions and assist the individuals that helped to usher in the recession.

And yet.

Morality has never been a relative matter. It's not about being as ethical as the next person. It's about living true to your own norms and beliefs. If anything, we live in a culture that permits or even encourages lifestyles that are not especially...honest, to tell the truth. We might fudge on our taxes, drive above the speed limit, tell little white lies, or even interpret our marriage vows liberally. Unfortunately, the people who are often the most influential in terms of setting standards of morality in our society are not the religious leaders or philosophers. Instead, they are frequently politicians, entertainers, and athletes, who disavow their responsibility as role models but whose actions—which are sometimes morally disturbing—influence many people. So who are *we* going to be?

When we set healthy, appropriate behavioral norms for ourselves and live up to those expectations, we feel good. When we don't live up to those values, we feel bad. And when we feel bad about ourselves, we often mask those feelings by justifying our behavior or by burying our feelings under a haze of alcohol, cigarette smoke, drugs, overeating, gambling, or any of the "isms" that afflict our society. Even worse, feeling bad about ourselves can interfere with our ability to pray wholeheartedly for help.

Every day, we are confronted with moral and ethical choices, big and small. Life isn't perfect; holding ourselves to impossible standards of morality is just as bad as holding ourselves to no standards at all. The dilemma becomes this: How can we be the best possible person without making ourselves crazy in the process? To put it simply, the issue is this: Keeping secrets requires a great deal of energy. We need that same energy in order to live our lives to the fullest, as well as to protect our most precious asset—our health.

We have a choice. We can use our life energy or life force to keep secrets…or we can use it to stay healthy. Maintaining immunity from acts we know are wrong helps us maintain our immunity against illness and disease. And we need that same energy to keep generating the hope and optimism human beings require in order to maximize the quality of life. If we think something is wrong, it's always best not to do it.

If you're doing something you aren't proud of, now is the time to stop. If you're having trouble stopping and you think that your negative behavior pattern may have crossed the line into addiction, contact a support group such as Alcoholics Anonymous (A.A.) or talk to a therapist and get help. The better we live as moral beings, the better we live and, once again, the higher our resilience to stress becomes.

Come to terms with God.

I am deeply impressed with the model of spirituality in A.A. because it works so magnificently for those who suffer from that terrible disease. As a physician, I must admit I have never been successful helping alcoholics unless they went to A.A. And like most physicians in our society, I know very little about what does work with alcoholics, other than finding a spiritual path.

A.A. requires no specific allegiance to any type of organized religion, but it does suggest in the strongest possible term that its members meditate and pray. To whom? To a Higher Power or God of their own choosing. Some people experience discomfort praying to the God of the religion in which they were raised. If you are one of those individuals, you can benefit by redefining God in any way you like...as long as your definition of your Higher Power comprises Love and Compassion. By doing so, you can follow one religion, many religions, or no religion at all, as long as you remain in regular contact with the God of your understanding.

Many of us struggle, of course, with what's called "theodicy" (pronounced thee-ODD-uh-see)—the question of how God could permit bad things to happen to good people. This question in and of itself keeps many people from seeking to have a relationship with any concept of God, one of their own making, one they grew up with, or one they write about in school.

The best answer I can offer is this: What separates human beings from animals or plants is the fact that we have the freedom to choose to do the right thing or the wrong thing. We have the power to choose to do the right thing or the wrong thing, and unless we are truly sociopathic, we know the difference between right and wrong.

As for tragedy—the death of a child, God forbid, or something equally horrific—tragedy can be a profound teacher. And the existence of tragedy, as inexplicable as it is, does not automatically point to the nonexistence of God.

I hope this helps to resolve some conflicts you might have about who or what God is. If not, I would urge you to continue the inquiry. As the expression goes, the way to find God is to seek God.

Pray and meditate.

The good news is that by this point in our evolution as a society, it no longer seems altogether surprising for a medical doctor to recommend meditation and prayer. Are there happy people who neither meditate nor pray? Undoubtedly. But you'll find that throughout history, often the happiest, most well grounded, and most successful people had a strong reliance on a Power greater than themselves.

So what about prayer and meditation? What do these terms mean? Prayer simply means talking to God, and meditation means listening for God's answer. These skills are important when times are good…and vital when times are challenging, as they are abundantly so today because of economic challenges, terrorism, and other issues.

Here are my own personal steps to having a successful experience with prayer:

Step 1. Pray as if God were listening.
Step 2. Repeat step 1.
Step 3. Repeat steps 1 and 2.

People ask, "Why should I pray? Does God really need our prayers?" God isn't likely changed when we pray. But *we* are. We are changed in that we are reminded that there is something bigger than ourselves in the world, that our problems are not the biggest things in the world, and that we are not alone.

I'm always moved by the 23rd Psalm, especially the line that states, "Thou preparest a table before me in the presence of mine enemies; Thou hast anointed my head with oil; my cup runneth over." To me, this means we have to keep our robe as pure white as possible in order to pray wholeheartedly to God. In other words, don't be doing anything you think is wrong. Make your life a prayer, not just the words you speak to God.

And what about meditation?

We need to meditate because we're always busy in our heads planning, reflecting, worrying, strategizing, or just thinking. Meditation means stilling our thoughts so we can enjoy the peace of mind that we enjoyed as children. When we meditate, we unchain ourselves from the past and future and instead anchor ourselves firmly in the present. We pass through the gateway of our soul to experience inner peace. As poet Robert Browning wrote, "There is an inmost center in us all/Where truth abides in fullness." Meditation gets us there.

The medical benefits from meditation remove it from the realm of concepts that may seem too foreign or vague. When we meditate...

- The body's internal pharmacy and internal healing force are stimulated.
- The brain's electrical activity is calmed through an increase in brain waves associated with deep relaxation.
- The body's metabolic rate slows down, leading to more efficient oxygen consumption.
- Blood pressure and pulse rate both decrease, lessening the workload on the heart.

The most important thing to know about meditation is that nobody gets it perfect. Some people think that if they do not have the ability to banish all their thoughts from their mind, then they're meditating poorly. Nothing could be further from the truth. Meditation really amounts to deep, relaxed breathing, which allows you to calm down your brain waves, refocus and rebalance your energy, and take a brief, mental vacation from the stresses and strains of everyday life. Some people recommend meditating 20 to 30 minutes a day. I say that meditation is a lot like exercise—if you aren't familiar or comfortable with it, just do it for a few minutes each day. Practically anyone can find 5 minutes for this life-enhancing process.

There are many ways to meditate. Here's one simple way: Just sit comfortably, close your eyes, relax your shoulders, breathe slowly and deeply, and say to yourself over and over, "I have strength," or "I love you, God." Specific instructions for meditating can be found in the Epilogue.

You'll feel better within the first few breaths!

One of the natural reactions to stress is to hold your breath. That's because in hunter–gatherer times, a hunter would go completely silent, lest an animal hear him breathing and run away. When we get stressed today, our breathing still gets shallow, even though it doesn't really serve any physiological purpose. If anything, a stressful event or situation triggers shallow breathing, and the reduction of oxygen to the brain makes us feel worse and even more stressed-out, contributing to an even worse reaction in our brains about how to handle the situation.

Meditation, by contrast, elongates our breathing, increases our lung capacity, and makes us feel better and more alive…and not coincidentally, enables us to handle stressful situations more effectively. Stress happens only when we *think*. So if we can slow down or even stop our thought process—which could better be described as our *worry* process—we can help our minds achieve stillness. And by quieting our thoughts, or by expanding the time between thoughts, that's when we feel peace. During meditation, our bodies produce endorphins, nitric oxide, and other healing chemicals, which create positive changes in body and brain chemistry. Otherwise, we're reliving the past, fearing the future, worrying about the present…instead of enjoying what's great about our lives. That's the physiological and spiritual benefit of meditation!

If you've never meditated before, or if the idea of meditation sounds odd to you, then just try the short

Emergency Stress Meditation at the end of this book. You'll be suspending your concerns and worries for just a few minutes, but I'm sure you'll be convinced about the positive effect of meditation on your mood, energy, and outlook on life.

I've worked hard to craft some special meditations that are especially useful and helpful in these troubled economic times. They'll help you bring your Guardian Angels into your life. I invite you to try these meditations, because they come with my special guarantee: If they don't make you feel more relaxed, happier, and content, I'll cheerfully refund all of your stress!

Have fun!

It's amazing how human beings respond to unhappiness… by eliminating from their lives the things that actually make them happy!

When you're feeling good about yourself, it's important to do things that make you happy. When you're feeling down, it's ESSENTIAL!!! Quick quiz: When was the last time you got a massage? Or went swimming? Or read a good book (aside from this one, of course!)? Our capacity for pleasure sometimes gets buried under a mountain of stress. So the easiest way to dig ourselves out is to stop fighting the wars against whatever stressors we're facing and instead do something just for fun. It might be enjoying nature by going for a hike or visiting a park or garden. It might be listening to some inspiring music, or watching an upbeat movie. (This is NOT the time to make yourself miserable with a real downer of a film, by the way.)

It might even be sitting down and enjoying a cup of tea—just plain old black tea, not necessarily the fancy or expensive kind. Drinking tea has always been a traditional remedy for relaxation and stress relief, and now, researchers in England (where else?) have found that tea drinkers tend to have lower levels of cortisol, which is commonly known as the "stress hormone." Cortisol is secreted by our adrenal glands, especially in response to fear and anxiety, and it can lead to health problems ranging all the way from weakened immunity to excess belly fat. So take tea and see.

Or just plain laugh. With today's amazing technology, laughter is just a few clicks away. Go to YouTube.com, punch in the name of your favorite comedian, and enjoy the physiological and psychological benefits of a good belly laugh or two. You'll thank me for this one. The main thing is that you don't always have to attack stressful situations in a direct head-to-head confrontation. Sneak around your stress by going to the beach, the forest, the comedy club, the concert hall, the ballgame, or the comedy download. Trust me—in 50 years of medicine, I have never heard of a patient who died laughing! Enjoy yourself—and then you'll find that your seemingly impossible problems might just have some solutions you never imagined.

And don't forget to smile at strangers. Some might think you're crazy…but some just might smile back.

So there you have it—a variety of ways to improve the quality of your breathing and the quality of your life. By exerting control over your movement, your breathing, and your environment, you're no longer that NASCAR vehicle chugging around and coming in last. Instead, you're leading the pack! And your ability to cope with life will continue to get stronger and stronger and stronger. That's why I say—and I hope you'll agree with me—that the good news is you've truly got more control of your life than you think, even now when life couldn't seem crazier or more upsetting. You truly do have the power to create your life anew.

*

TO CALL ON THE GUARDIAN ANGEL OF STRENGTH...

Take a few simple steps that create a sense of control over your life, health, and well-being. For example...get out and move! Create a healthier, more soothing environment for yourself at home and at work. Be a good, ethical person who cares for others. Meditate, pray, and engage yourself in the question of who or what God really is. The Angel of Strength will be there for you to help you take more control of your life.

CHAPTER 5

EATING RIGHT: FOOD FOR THOUGHT

Everything I like is illegal, immoral, or fattening.

—ALEXANDER WOOLLCOTT

When the going gets tough, the tough…go to the kitchen.

Or the fast-food store.

Or the freezer to look for some ice cream.

The problem with stressful times is that many of us turn to food for comfort and solace. Unfortunately, this is a case where our solutions can be even worse than our problems. People often overeat out of a sense of emotional despair, which creates a vicious cycle because they see themselves gaining weight…which leads to more despair…which leads to another trip to the refrigerator.

We cannot eat our way out of stress…but we can eat our way to health.

When we're overweight, we're actually stressing our bodies, which weren't meant to process that much food or carry that much fat around. So we can actually manage stress in our lives if we find a healthier way to eat. And we'll live longer and happier lives…which means that we'll get to survive this economic downturn and thrive, allowing us to see our children and grandchildren grow and live beautiful lives of their own.

And when we eat properly and shop in a healthy manner for our families, we're giving to ourselves and to our loved ones many wonderful gifts—the gift of nutrition, the gift of delicious, healthy food, and the gift of healthy and appropriate weight. We're also modeling for those we love a healthier way to cope with stress than to hit the drive-through line for another cheeseburger and chocolate shake.

The problem with fast foods and junk foods is that they may taste great…but they exact a price from our bodies. They're hard to digest and offer little nourishment. I'd like to share with you a strategy for eating that captures the energy we need each day. We've all heard of solar power for our homes. What we really need is solar power for our bodies! Healthy foods, like fruits and vegetables, are so important to eat because they are steeped in sunlight and capture energy from the sun. That "solar energy" inside these foods provides us the life energy we need to stay healthy. So let's examine some ways to get the energy we need from the food we eat, while reducing from our diets the kinds of food that do us more harm than good.

Here are some ways to think about food that will make a wonderful difference in your life right now.

Supermarket sweep.

Here's an experience for you that you might find enlightening and even entertaining. Go to the supermarket, pick out a couple of items to buy, and then get in line at the checkout counter behind a person who is noticeably overweight. (The unfortunate thing about American society is that it won't be that hard to find such a person, especially in the supermarket!)

Study carefully the items this person has in his or her cart. Chances are, you'll see a lot of processed foods, a lot of things that have high levels of sugar and salt, a lot of things that come in boxes and cans, and a lot of things that don't even look like real food! (Ever seen a Pringle tree? Or a Coca-Cola river? Or a field of...processed white flour?)

You don't have to say anything to that person. Just notice the kinds of food that people who are very overweight buy.

Now repeat the experiment, but this time, be sure to get in line behind someone who has an attractive, healthy body. The person doesn't have to look like a beauty queen or a movie star, only that the person looks healthy, appears to be maintaining a healthy weight, and probably takes good care of himself or herself. What's in that person's cart?

Chances are, you'll notice a lot of fruits and vegetables, healthy cereals, multigrain bread, fish and chicken, not too much red meat. What you probably *won't* see is the sort of stuff that our heavier-set friend purchased—things with high levels of sugar and salt; fancy, plastic juice boxes (never as healthy as the juice you get when you eat a piece of fruit); or snack foods that no one could really consider healthy, even if the labels say "fat-free." (Just because a product doesn't *contain* fat doesn't mean it won't *turn into* fat once it enters the body.)

Isn't it interesting that healthy people usually buy healthy foods and unhealthy people...don't?

Fill your tank with premium...and get the lead out!

If you think back to the NASCAR illustration in the previous chapter, we had a car that came in last because it wasn't getting the nutrition it needed—the gas and oil to keep it running. What's under your hood? What are you feeding yourself, and just as important, what are you feeding your family?

If you think of your body as a "food processor," it's happiest processing healthy things—fruits and vegetables, legumes, whole grains, fish and poultry. Red meat is really not that healthy for you. And if you're going to drink milk, make it low-fat or nonfat, and always try to get the freshest eggs you can.

Coincidentally, those healthy things I mentioned a moment ago are the sorts of things that our ancestors ate long before the introduction of white flour, white sugar, preservatives, chemicals, additives, trans fats, and other unhealthy ingredients that improve the taste of food but certainly don't make it very healthy. Healthy people increase their energy by eating healthy foods that are easy for their body to process and from which essential nutrients can be derived. People who aren't as healthy in their food choices pick things that actually drain the body's energy because they are harder to digest, create unhealthy levels of fat, and actually lower the body's ability to heal itself when it gets sick and prevent it from getting sick in the first place.

Another way to think about this is that people who are committed to their health mostly shop the perimeter of the supermarket—where they find the fruits, vegetables, legumes, nuts, healthier breads, fish, and poultry. People who aren't as healthy shop the inside aisles, where they find the cookies and crackers, soda and alcohol, ice cream and other frozen foods.

I admit this is an over-generalization, and there are certainly healthy things to be found in the center of the supermarket, just as there are unhealthy things, like pastry and other tasty delights, along the perimeter. But I think you get my point. Invite the Angel of Health to come into your life and help you put into your shopping cart only those foods that enhance your health. In so doing, you will have eliminated one of the most basic stresses on the body—the obligation that so many of us put on our bodies to process foods that the body simply does not desire.

You may notice on television that commercials for over-the-counter antiacid medications feature unhealthy looking actors and actresses playing "regular folks" who discover that with medication, they can eat pizza dripping with grease. I find these commercials disturbing. It is important to remember that many of these medications may have harmful side effects for some of us. Moreover, we need to question the ethics of these commercials, which give people the impression that if they take pills (which may have unwanted side effects), they can then eat unhealthy foods (which also have unwanted side effects).

Another problem with the commercial marketing of medications is that it makes people overly worried about rare disease, and thus they feel the need to buy medication they might not necessarily need. Restless leg syndrome? It's so rare that I've never seen it in 50 years of practicing medicine. Overactive bladder? How about overactive marketing? Moreover, sleeping pills are being marketed relentlessly. It is also important to note that the drugs marketed to cure these marketed diseases also have side effects. You know why I call these new medications wonder drugs? Because I wonder if those drugs are actually necessary for your health.

Go live!

Another way to think about what goes into your shopping cart is the distinction between "live" foods and "dead" foods. Live foods come primarily from the soil and are still able to transmit life energy from the sun. Relatively dead foods, such as red meat, whole milk, and nutritionally empty beverages like soda and alcohol, clog your system. Keep your system running clean by choosing a preponderance of live foods for your diet.

When it comes to live foods, it's best to favor fruits and vegetables, giving particular emphasis to food that is locally grown and in season. The greater the distance that food travels, the more nutrients and taste that get sacrificed along the way. In addition, it takes a certain amount of jet fuel or truck fuel to bring produce a long way, adding to the reasons why organic and locally grown are the best kinds of fruits and vegetables to eat—they're the best for us and for the planet.

After fruits and vegetables, it's important to favor legumes, such as peas and beans, and complex carbohydrates, such as brown rice, nuts, and whole grains. That old Wonder Bread ad told us that it grew our bodies in 12 ways. Unfortunately, that claim holds no nutritional value. Most bread made with white flour is less healthy, because it has been stripped of the nutrients that make bread worth eating, earning it the sobriquet "the staff of life."

The next step down the healthy food ladder is where you'll find fresh fish, poultry, and eggs, which are still considerably better for you than red meat. As much as possible, you want to eat food that has never had a face or a mother. In other words, you may want to control your carnivore instincts and hence limit your intake of red meat and, to a lesser degree, fish and poultry. It's best to remove from our diets most of the simple carbohydrates (pastries, candy, and such) and anything artificial, because as we've already discussed, it takes your body more energy to digest these foods than your body receives from having eaten them.

If you're hungry, drink water instead of snacking!

Think about this: Your body is 92 percent water. So it needs to have its water level replenished every day. This involves drinking a great deal of water, far more than most people do—at least eight glasses a day. (Coffee doesn't count; It's a diuretic, which means that it actually draws water out of your system instead of adding vital water to it.) In addition to drinking water, we also need to eat a preponderance of foods that contain a high level of water. One of the reasons why fruits and vegetables are so important is that they have a very high water content.

Foods like meat, bread, doughnuts, ice cream, and other snack foods may taste good and actually contain some nutritional benefit (but not much compared with a grapefruit). Yet these foods have a low—or even zero—water content. As I suggested a moment ago, everything you eat either cleanses your system...or clogs it. It all comes back to the choices you make at the supermarket. So shop the perimeter; aim for foods that come from the soil and are locally grown and in season; avoid the things that will make you and your family fat; and drink enough water to meet your body's needs. Check out a farmer's market and find out how delicious fresh fruits and veggies can be.

Don't buy into the myths about food.

You might think human beings can only be healthy if they eat lots and lots of beef, pork, and chicken. Today's television media certainly promotes meat consumption. However, in reality, you don't need as much meat as you might think. Protein from animals is not required for energy or health.

To lose weight, you don't have to count calories. As long as you're limiting or, better still, avoiding the saturated fats found in meats and processed foods like doughnuts or cake, you don't have to monitor how many grams of carbs, protein, and fats you're taking in. Listen to your body; it knows what it wants—healthy foods from the top of the food ladder. Give yourself what your body needs, not what your sugar cravings call for to help excess pounds melt away.

Some sugars are better than others. Fruit is bursting with life energy, but a candy bar is dead. Healthy sugars are found in whole fruits. Simple sugars, found in processed snack foods, turn quickly to fat in the human body.

Eat before eight. If you finish your eating for the day by 8:00 P.M., you will sleep more soundly and thus store up healthful energy. If you're an early-to-bed type, have your last meal two hours before bedtime. And the best late-night snack isn't pizza or potato chips; it's fresh fruit.

Cow's milk is best for baby cows, not for people. (Think about that.) Humans are the only species that drinks the milk of another species. We don't need cow's milk for our health. Where do you get your calcium? From the soil, with veggies and fruits.

Plant foods capture the energy of the sun. They are the synthesis of life energy that allows your body to absorb the sun's rays. Meat and animal products contain little sunlight.

They have poor life energy and may actually speed up the aging process because they require so much energy to digest. But I fear you won't hear about any of these concepts in the ads you see on TV.

And remember the most important (and most widely ignored) piece of guidance that I or anyone else can offer you about healthy eating…portion control, portion control, portion control! In other words, eat only what you need to eat, not everything you feel like eating!

Choose the right supplements.

As a health expert, I recognize that in today's world, it is simply impossible for even the healthiest eater to derive all the nutrients that he or she needs just from food and drink. In my opinion, it is highly unlikely that we can get the optimum benefits of vitamins and minerals from just the foods we eat. The authors of a major review in the *Journal of the American Medical Association* conclude, "Most people do not consume an optimal amount of all vitamins by diet alone. Pending strong evidence of effectiveness from randomized trials, it appears prudent for all adults to take vitamin supplements."[1] Therefore, it seems no longer optional but truly essential to supplement your food with appropriate vitamins and minerals.

---

1. *Journal of the American Medical Association*, June 19, 2002, Vol. 287, No. 23, pg. 3127.

For your nutritional supplement, you need a balanced, comprehensive daily supplement that provides all the vitamins and minerals your body needs. Ideally, you want to look for a supplement that contains vitamin B complex and antioxidants, including vitamin C, CoQ10, and alpha-lipoic acid.

So the next time you go shopping, don't shop alone. Be sure to invite the Angel of Health to guide you to make the healthiest choices at the supermarket. This will enable you to recreate your body into one that can withstand the negative effects of stress as never before.

*

TO CALL ON THE GUARDIAN ANGEL OF HEALTH...

Notice what healthy people put into their shopping carts. Use the distinction of live versus "dead" foods to help you decide what to buy and what to eat. Drink enough water to stay hydrated, and drink water when you think you're hungry (you might really just be thirsty). Don't let stress make you hit the fast-food restaurants or the ice-cream store. Take control of your health by shopping right, eating right, and taking the necessary nutritional supplementation.

CHAPTER 6

STRESS: IT'S ABOUT TIME

The sooner I fall behind, the more time I have to catch up.

—ANONYMOUS

For many of us, time seems to be speeding by more quickly than ever before. We're more concerned than ever about the fact that there just aren't enough hours in the day to do all the things we need or want to do. And that's especially true now, when many people are working two or even three jobs just to stay afloat.

Work is taking up more and more of our lives, and with the advent of BlackBerrys and iPhones, the wall of separation that once existed between work and home has come tumbling down. And it has landed smack on our marriages and families. The time that we used to be able to devote uninterruptedly to our loved ones must now be shared. Ours is a world where an increasing number of workers must be available to their employers day and night, sometimes even on weekends and vacations. And for those seeking employment, the job hunt has only gotten more difficult as fewer employers are hiring in today's economic climate and there are more competitors than ever for any given job.

Even for those who are not slaves to the workplace, there still never seems to be enough time. Our lives, and the lives of our children, seem busier than ever, and when parents aren't driving kids from one activity to the next, they're often struggling to keep up with the other requirements of family life—finding time (and money) to pay the bills, keep the house clean, and keep up with maintenance tasks. Some retirees and others on fixed incomes are finding it increasingly stressful to make ends meet when their life savings and/or pensions are in jeopardy...or in freefall.

Not surprisingly, lack of time has turned into a major source of stress for millions of Americans. And somehow, paradoxically, the busier we get, the less we get done, and the more stress we feel because of all the things we have left undone.

How do you reverse this glum trend? How do you create a sense of peacefulness with regard to the limitations you face, including the fact there are just 24 hours in a day?

Earlier, I mentioned the two San Francisco cardiologists who, in the early 1960s, coined the term "Type A behavior." They demonstrated that the frenetic pace that Type A people display is a serious contributing factor to heart attacks, hypertension, strokes, and other potentially fatal illnesses. One of the terms they created to describe this issue is "hurry sickness"—the compulsive need to accomplish more and more things in fewer and fewer moments.

Despite being aware that Type A behavior can be dangerous to one's health, more and more of us display those same Type A characteristics. We often hurry other people when they speak, sometimes even finishing sentences for them out of an impatience that comes when the other person doesn't get to the point quickly enough. Our technological means of communicating have reduced opportunities for the casual, friendly conversation we used to enjoy as a matter of course each day, instead cutting to the chase with texted pieces of information unembellished by even the most casual "How are you today?" As a result, practically all of us have experienced problems in business or personal relationships when an e-mail or text (or perhaps now an entry on a Facebook page or a comment on Twitter) is misunderstood.

We're driving faster, more prone to road rage, less likely to let the other driver in. Increasingly, we take the normal "slings and arrows" of everyday life as personal affronts that require us to respond, often violently. Parents are less likely to involve their children in organized sports because they fear the overreaction of the "nightmare dad" or even the "nightmare mom," who can't tolerate the idea that their perfect little Jimmy isn't getting the maximum amount of playing time. Things have reached such a point that violence, even fatal violence, has broken out among parents over the most insignificant of disputes.

And even if we somehow remain relatively calm behind the wheel and don't engage with other parents on the sidelines of our kids' soccer, Pop Warner, and Little League games, we still feel rushed both as individuals and as a society. As one country music song puts it, "I'm always running…and always running behind." In these times, even some older folks are running around at a frenetic pace, because they're worried about how they will survive economically and pay for their increasingly expensive health care.

The stress that we experience from rushing through our lives has a definite negative effect on our health and, at the same time, it makes us less resilient when other stressful events occur in our lives. It becomes harder and harder for us to respond calmly instead of reacting abruptly when we are challenged or faced with conflict. "Hurry sickness" touches our psyches, our health and well-being, our marriages and families, our income, and our well-being. We're becoming frenzied trying to protect our assets, while forgetting that health is our single most precious asset.

So how can the Angel of Time come to our rescue and relieve us of this intense time pressure that so many of us face?

Do less.

This may seem surprising, because you might expect me to offer you guidance on how to accomplish more in the limited amount of time you have each day. Instead, I'd like you to actually do fewer things! Books about time management suggest that people keep a diary of how they spend each hour for a day or a week. The problem is that people whose lives are too busy just don't have the time to write that kind of diary! But if you're like most people, you simply don't have all the time you might desire to accomplish all the things you wish to do.

So instead of trying to make a list of all your current activities, which would only add to your stress, allow me to invite you to do at least one less thing than you are currently doing. Think for a moment about where in your life you are spending valuable time on something that you could possibly live without. Again, think about getting away from the TV and computer screens that are mental vampires, sucking the life out of us by stealing our time and attention.

In an earlier chapter, I recommended turning off the TV long enough for a family to have dinner together and shutting down all technology long enough for a couple to find intimate time. Now I'm making a slightly different suggestion—devote less time, perhaps radically less time, to channel surfing and Web surfing and instead use that time for the sorts of activities I mentioned earlier that actually enhance your ability to handle stress, such as shopping for healthy foods, getting off the couch and moving, reading a good book, or simply getting caught up on some of those nagging tasks around the house that somehow never manage to get done.

By doing less and by carefully choosing which activities give you the least amount of benefit for the time commitment they require, you'll actually end up creating more time in your day. And that in and of itself will reduce the stress level in your life.

Talk positively about time.

Our subconscious mind cannot tell the difference between reality and what we *say* is reality. Studies have shown that approximately 5 percent of our mental efforts take place on a conscious level, and as much as 95 percent of what we think about happens on an unconscious level. So the 5 percent of the time that you're consciously thinking about something is when you are giving instructions to your subconscious brain about what is real in your life. So here's the question: What are you telling your subconscious is true?

If you're like most people, your conscious mind is telling your subconscious mind that "There isn't enough time," "There isn't enough money," "I can never get done everything I need to do," and other self-defeating, negative statements and beliefs. The problem is that we as human beings buy into the negative statements we tell ourselves, and we make those negative statements our reality. In other words, if we tell ourselves we don't have enough time or enough money, then we probably won't. That's because your subconscious mind is going to do everything possible it can to make you a truth teller instead of a liar. And if the truth you say is that you don't have enough time, your subconscious mind will find a million ways to rob you of whatever time you need in order to get done the things you need to do.

So the solution is to quit telling yourself all those negative things about time (and about money, and love, and anything else, for that matter). In his classic work, *As a Man Thinketh,* James Allen wrote more than a century ago that the mind is like a garden, where positive thoughts are like flowers and negative thoughts are like weeds. We all know how weeds can overtake a garden, so it is our job constantly to notice and uproot any negative thoughts in the garden that is our mind. As a result, positive thoughts can take root, bloom, and create the beauty that we need in order to enjoy our lives to the fullest. So weed out the negative thoughts that you notice cropping up and focus on the positives in your life.

If you hear yourself saying, "I don't have enough time," then say, and preferably out loud, "I have all the time I need for all the things I need to do." Making a declaration like that has a relaxing and liberating effect on every one of the 80 trillion cells in your body. It's a wonderful way to relieve tension.

The main point here is to stop telling yourself negative things about time, so you can go on and function in a manner that provides you with a sense of peacefulness as you go through your busy day.

Prioritize.

As the expression goes, Life's hard by the yard, but it's a cinch by the inch. Most of us place overwhelming, impossible demands on ourselves, or we expect far too little of ourselves. The goal is to hit the "sweet spot," where our expectations of what we can accomplish in any given 24-hour period are in line with reality, where we are neither asking too much nor too little of ourselves in a given day. The best suggestion I can share with you, with regard to time management, is simply to make a list of the four things that you would like to accomplish today. Keep the list with you and stay with each item until you have completed it. Then go to the next item on your list and repeat the process. Keep doing this until you've gotten to the end of your list.

Some people respond negatively to this suggestion because they like to multitask or jump from one project to the other. The simple fact is that our brains do not like to shunt between tasks—that every interruption costs us in terms of time, focus, and quality of effort. So it's best to stay with one task and see it to completion and then move on to the next. And if you're afraid that you won't accomplish all four things, well, that's why they invented tomorrow! Often, we put so much time pressure on ourselves to accomplish things that really could be done tomorrow or the next day. I'm not suggesting that you use this concept as an excuse for procrastination or laziness. I am saying that if you can manage your tasks—whether you are a homemaker, a business person, a factory worker, or a retiree—into manageable chunks, you are far more likely to be accomplished and productive, and once again, you will have reduced the amount of stress in your life.

A word about multitasking. Many people pride themselves on their ability to do many different things at the same time. In fact, multitasking is one of the key stressors that may actually make people more prone to heart attacks, strokes, and other debilitating and fatal illnesses. Generally speaking, the brain was simply never wired to multitask. We cannot, in a healthful, life-enhancing way, do too many things at the same time. In so doing, we create incredible amounts of stress for ourselves.

We think we are reducing stress by accomplishing more than one thing at a time, when in fact, by doing so, we are causing ourselves more stress than ever. So my gentle but strong suggestion to you is to abandon multitasking to your personal computer. Do one thing at a time, do it well, and move on to the next item on your list. That's the best way to regain a sense of control over time.

Create a more peaceful environment for yourself at home and at work.

Most of us live lives surrounded by clutter. I know the old joke that a clean car is the sign of a sick mind. But actually, the reverse is true. When our homes, our workplaces, and our vehicles have a sense of orderliness to them, we actually feel more peaceful and less stressed out. Most of us tend to leave stacks of papers and bills in plain sight, and every time we see them, something inside us just clenches and says, "When am I going to find the time to get that done?" Conversely, when we keep our desks—at home and at work—and the rest of our living spaces orderly and clutter-free, we have a sense of peacefulness and accomplishment. This acts as a powerful counterweight to the trouble and conflict we encounter every time we pay attention to the news.

You might say, "Well then, when am I supposed to pay the bills?" You can pay them once or twice a month, or you can pay them as they arrive. The key thing is to keep your bills and all your other papers and documents, important and otherwise, out of plain sight. Think about a Zen monastery. Any stacks of papers, old magazines, or other distractions come to mind? Of course not. They keep it neat, because neat increases peace!

A side benefit of keeping your personal space clutter-free is that it's easier to find things, like your keys, for example. If everything is everywhere, then it can be very hard to put your hands on what you need at any given moment. And we've all gone through the agony of trying to rush out the door when we can't find our car keys, wallet, or purse. I'm not saying you have to be fanatical about neatness, because that can tend toward its own form of insanity! I am suggesting that you exercise power over your environment by committing to keeping it neat and orderly, and this will increase the peace in your mind and in your heart.

Having written this, however, I'm not myself a paragon of neatness! Yet I know how much my stress is reduced when I reduce the clutter level on and around my desk!

Rest.

Triathlons are races with three components—swimming, bicycling, and running. The joke among triathletes is that the hardest activity for competitors in those races is to rest.

It's not just true of triathletes—it's true for all of us. In today's society of endless motion and frenetic activity, many of us feel guilty if we think about sitting down for a moment. There's just so much to do! And yet, the body was never geared for the 24/7/365 lifestyle that technology imposes upon us. The e-mails just keep coming. So do the phone messages. So do the texts. The natural impetus is to respond to everything as soon as it arrives. But what about our responding to our need for sleep?

One of the greatest threats to health in modern society is sleep deprivation. We're so busy with technology or just trying to keep up with our lives that few of us get the deep, restful sleep we need in order for our bodies to carry on the repair work necessary to keep us healthy and happy. Every time we add another activity or responsibility to our lives, we generally take the time for that activity out of our sleep. Before long, carrying on without sleep will catch up with us, causing all sorts of health disorders, including a terrible sense of frustration and stress.

So getting enough rest on any given night is an absolute necessity for all of us. We also need to eliminate from our life "sleep stealers," like alcohol, caffeine, or nicotine, before bedtime. If you need something to help you fall asleep, try a cup of chamomile tea instead of a "hot toddy." Keep in mind that alcohol in any quantity in the evening tends to keep older folks awake or wake them in the middle of the night.

We need to respect the body's rhythms and find ways to shut down for a day. In the Judeo-Christian tradition, we find the concept of the Sabbath, a day in which no productive work is done. The Bible recommends this as a way of life because it gives us a chance to step back from the eternal tumult that is our lives, gain perspective, enjoy the company of loved ones, and "get off the clock." Today, we divide time into smaller and smaller fragments. When we take a full day for ourselves, we free ourselves from the tyranny of time and can enjoy a long meal, a nap, a walk, or a deep conversation with our loved ones. By stinting on taking a day of rest, in any form, we are robbing ourselves of the healthful, relaxing benefits of allowing our bodies—and our lives—to slow down.

We can take a lesson from some of the great athletes of the world, especially tennis players. Athletes who cannot rest successfully, seldom stay at the top of their game for long. We all need daily rest, we need work breaks, and to the extent that we can find ways to do so, we need a day of rest. Most of us constantly have our fingers on the fast-forward button, when we really need to hit the pause button for a while. Naps are terrific at any age. If anything, more rest deters us from pushing our mental panic button, especially in the present economy. Take time to reclaim the way time works in your life. Your stress will diminish, and your enjoyment of life will soar.

Here are some practical ways to bring the Angel of Time into your life:

Wear a smile. No matter what you've lost or what you are concerned about, the best thing you can wear is a smile, because it makes you look better than everyone around you, and it makes you feel better about yourself.

The real key is connecting. Partner up with those you love and who love you. Deepen friendships and seek more. Let those in your circle know you need help! They need your example to admit to their own pain!

Take a real vacation. Take an emotional vacation from worrying—for a day, a weekend, or a week, *especially* when there is nothing you can do about things anyway.

Break up routine. Take nature walks, do a crossword puzzle, look at old photos with others. Don't lose your libido—or at least talk about it with your loved one or doctor if that is an issue.

Treat yourself nicely. Acknowledge efforts; at least reward yourself by saying, "Atta girl" or "Atta boy!"...or at the end of each day, write down your thoughts in a journal.

*

TO CALL ON THE GUARDIAN ANGEL OF TIME...

Do less. The more you pack into a day, the more frustrating the day becomes. Prioritize—pick no more than four things you need to accomplish in a given day, and stay with each one until you finish it, avoiding multitasking and distraction as much as you possibly can. And finally, rest. Give yourself the pauses during the day, the rest at night, and where possible, complete days of rest so that you can be refreshed, happy, and above all, stress-free as you handle the many responsibilities of modern life.

CHAPTER 7

LOOKING FOR LOVE
IN ALL THE RIGHT PLACES

The hand that opens to give is open to receive.

—ANONYMOUS

There's an old saying that if everybody put their problems in a big pile in the middle of a room and got to see everyone else's problems, each person would walk out with the same set of problems that he or she brought in.

Whenever I think about that story, I always wonder why you have to take any problems at all with you! Why not just leave your problems in that room, along with everybody else's?

To be alive, however, is to face problems, big and small. We have pebble-in-the-shoe-size challenges, and then we have really serious issues affecting the health or even the physical or economic survival of our loved ones and ourselves. Indeed, as the Reverend Norman Vincent Peale wrote, the only people who have no problems are in the cemeteries. And at a time in his life when he had few problems to speak of, Peale looked up at the heavens and said, "God, don't you trust me anymore?"

Some of us view problems as challenges to be faced with vigor and great expectations of success. And at other times, our problems seem to overwhelm us, appearing to be too large for us to handle in any meaningful way. One of the most stressful things in life comes when problems or challenges occur at the same time or quickly in succession. It's wearing to have to face a lot of major issues all at once, and yet there's no way of predicting what we will have to face, when, or in what order. We simply do the best we can.

Perhaps the biggest problem that so many people in our society face has nothing to do with money or health. It has to do with the absence of love in their lives. When we don't love, when we can't love, we suffer. We suffer loneliness and a nagging sense of disconnection and even uselessness. Truly, I believe human beings were placed on this Earth to love life, to love each other, and to love our Creator. The health problems associated with an absence of love are so multitudinous that I've come to believe the word "ILL" actually stands for these three not-so-little words—I Lack Love. So in this chapter, I want to discuss with you how to make the all-important and healing move from I Lack Love to I Love Life.

So how exactly do you go about doing that?

In Alcoholics Anonymous, when a newly sober individual deems himself or herself ready for a relationship, the sponsor or mentor figure is likely to say, tongue in cheek, "First get a plant. Then get a dog. Then get into a relationship."

It's sage advice. When it comes to making connections, especially when we haven't done so successfully in the past, baby steps are the key. If you can take care of a plant, you can probably take care of a pet. And if you can demonstrate the responsibility that it takes to care for an animal, then you might just be ready to step up and get into a relationship.

We've discussed intimacy as one of the casualties of the stress-filled lifestyle we live today. The best definition I've ever seen for intimacy cannot be found in any dictionary. It is simply this: Intimacy means being yourself with someone else. It means not having to put up a front, or stand on your tippy-toes, or pretend to be something you are not. People who have the capacity for intimacy are able to show themselves—all of themselves, even their imperfections—to another person, secure in the knowledge that they will not be rejected for those imperfections. And if rejection occurs, it's most likely a reflection on the other person.

Another definition for intimacy is *into me, see*. In other words, intimacy is an invitation to others to see ourselves as we truly are.

One of the greatest frustrations of modern life is that for all the dating websites and social networking options, along with the more traditional means of meeting people, it seems harder and harder for true love to take root and successful relationships to flourish. How do we reverse that trend in our own lives? Granted, relationships have their own stresses built in. Indeed, as the expression goes, "Being in a relationship is like pouring Miracle-Gro on your character defects." And the great philosopher Baron de Montesquieu once compared people in relationships to mosquitoes at a screen door: Those who are in one want to get out, and those who are not in one want to get in.

But all kidding aside, most people who are experiencing the stress of loneliness would trade that unhappiness for the stresses and strains of a true love relationship. You can get a plant, and you can get a pet. But there is one more way to open your heart to prepare for love, and this stress-reducing way of life can also make a substantial difference for those who are already blessed with the gift of love in their lives.

In a word, I'm talking about service.

There are only two kinds of love in the world. There's personal love, which we bestow upon our spouse, our partner, our parents, our children, and our friends—people to whom we are connected by blood, marriage, community, or time.

Then there's another kind of love that we can bestow upon the world—impersonal love. Here, the recipient is not necessarily someone we chose or even knew before they came into our lives to receive our love. Impersonal love is the love we extend to those to whom we are of service.

There are countless ways to be of service to others. We can volunteer. We can serve as mentors. We can teach English as a second language. Even out-of-work bankers can counsel people on their finances. We can join AmeriCorps or the Peace Corps or some other organization that fosters goodwill and good works. We can serve in our religious institutions.

And the best kind of charitable giving we can provide, according to the Jewish physician and philosopher, Maimonides, is when the other person isn't aware of who her benefactor is…and doesn't even realize she's receiving charity!

How we serve is less important than the fact *that* we serve. It has long been proven that a fascinating parallel exists between what happens in our bodies on a chemical level when we serve others—when we bestow impersonal love—and when we get exercise. Our body's amazing internal chemistry fires off the same pleasant chemical reaction when we help others as it does when we work out. Long-distance runners will tell you that they experience the "runner's high." People who serve others will tell you that they experience what has been called the "helper's high."

From a neurological or biochemical perspective, there's little difference between the way the human body responds when it exercises its muscles and when it exercises its capacity to share love, caring, and warmth with others. I find this fascinating.

The parallel extends even further. Those who exercise on a long-term, continuous basis will tell you that they simply feel well most of the time. They are immune, by and large, to the aches, pains, and strains that the rest of us suffer on an occasional or even ongoing basis. Scientists have discovered that there are long-term, beneficial effects for those who exercise on a long-term, regular basis. It's not just that they feel better—that feeling of wellness is grounded in incontrovertible biochemical fact.

Intriguingly, individuals who serve others on a regular basis enjoy the same sense of well-being and wholeness that the long-term athletes enjoy. Just as there is a short-term benefit to being of service once in a while, there is a long-term payoff to making the act and art of caring for others a part of one's ongoing lifestyle. Just as there is a short-term and long-term runner's high, so too there is a short-term and long-term helper's high.

What does that tell us about the way human beings are created? It suggests that we are hardwired to take care of each other. This is a fact related to the phenomenon of survival of the fittest. On a cellular level and on a soul level, we thrive when we give of ourselves, just as on a muscular and skeletal level our bodies thrive when we exercise. I find this fact striking. I bring it up because loneliness is a stressful state in and of itself.

If loneliness weren't so displeasing, then you wouldn't have 20 million members on a single dating website and millions more searching for love on every corner of the Internet. Dinner for two sounds romantic; table for one sounds lonely. I'm not suggesting that it's unhealthy to enjoy one's own company or to find pleasure in solitude. At a time when people are so worried about economic survival, the idea of taking care of others seems outlandish. But service is even more important for our own psyches and our communities in hard times than when the economy is strong.

The way we make the surprising journey from I Lack Love to I Love Life, therefore, is by recognizing that what may be missing from our lives isn't some Japanese ivy or a cocker spaniel. Instead, the surest path to eliminating the stress of loneliness is to seek out opportunities to serve others in whatever way appeals to us the most. When we learn to bestow impersonal love on our fellows, we are actually training ourselves to improve at giving personal love, as well as receiving personal love from our spouses and those in our immediate personal lives.

At this point, you might be saying, "Dr. Taub, I just read a chapter dealing with the fact that I don't have enough time for my life as it is. And now you want me to find time every week to volunteer?"

That's exactly what I'm suggesting. No matter how busy you are, you can still carve out a few hours a week to give love to others, to be of service. A major reason is that if you can make this commitment to others, you'll get to see firsthand the problems that other people face. While you may help them with the guidance, care, and love that you have to share, they are going to help you even more, because they are going to help put your own problems into perspective.

Remember that initial comment I made at the beginning of the chapter about putting all our problems and cares in the middle of a room? Unless we are actively engaged in service work, it is all but impossible for us to know what problems other people are facing. We might see some statistics on the news, but no statistic has the power of meeting someone face to face who is suffering from a problem that that individual cannot change or cure. It takes the caring and warmth of a volunteer, a mentor, a sponsor, a teacher, or any other individual who is working without compensation to share impersonal love and service with others to make the critical difference in an individual's life. And when we actually see the problems of other people, suddenly our problems appear much smaller…if they don't disappear from the forefront of our minds altogether.

As the expression goes, when we're wrapped up in ourselves, we make a very small package. When we work with others and see that they are surviving somehow, perhaps with less money, fewer creature comforts, or even without many of the basics that we take for granted, like a roof over our heads or three meals a day, we begin to ask ourselves what we were so concerned about in the first place. The act of service in our communities allows us to exercise our muscle of caring, which is why I invite you to call upon the Angel of Compassion to come into your life and guide you to the appropriate service position for you. What's amazing is that so many people have so many different weaknesses, but on the other side of the coin, there are other individuals who possess the corresponding strengths necessary to help those suffering to overcome their weaknesses.

Sometimes individuals who continuously deal with extremely stressful situations like oncologists or hospice nurses, or those who care for infants or terminally ill relatives, can burn out. When you experience "compassion fatigue," slow down, follow the suggestions in this book, and be more of service to yourself. Take your walks. Eat in a healthy way.

Meditate and pray. Seek balance and rejuvenation, especially if you are the caregiver.

What strengths will you bring to the table? They are undoubtedly different from mine and from any other person on the planet. Your contribution is so unique that no one else can make it for you. And unless you are willing to take the time and effort to help create a better life for those around you, you'll never get to experience the remarkable benefits of service or impersonal love to others. The primary benefits, as we have seen, are comparing our problems with those of other people and, in so doing, diminishing the power our problems have over us. In addition, we get to benefit from that wondrous physiological reaction, short-term and long-term, that we get to enjoy when we share our time and love with others.

Again, it may seem paradoxical that in one chapter, I am inviting you to do less, and in this chapter, I am suggesting that you take on an added time commitment. But I think you'll agree that the magic comes when we take some of the focus off our own lives and place our energy, time, wisdom, and resources at the disposal of individuals whom we almost certainly would never otherwise have met.

And as the saying goes, "Don't put too much oxygen into your current set of problems, because in 90 days, you'll have a whole new set of things to worry about."

That may be true, but once you get yourself into the service lifestyle, the things that used to stress you out will seem much less important, much less relevant, and much less insurmountable than in the past. This is the journey from isolation to togetherness, from I Lack Love to I Love Life. What can you do for others? The investment of time and caring that you make will pay rich dividends in terms of your capacity to cope with stress...and just as important, to enjoy real love.

*

TO CALL ON THE GUARDIAN ANGEL OF COMPASSION...

Commit at least a few hours a week to serve others, and watch your problems diminish, as if by magic.

CHAPTER 8

MOVING BEYOND FEAR

You miss 100 percent of the shots you never take.

— HOCKEY LEGEND WAYNE GRETZKY

At its very core, stress *is* fear. Fear of the unknown, fear of tomorrow, fear of failure, fear of loss, fear of the uncontrollable. Fear is the absence of God or the lack of belief in a Higher Power for Good. Understanding the fear factor is the alpha and omega of identifying, preventing, managing, and curing stress.

FDR gave America heart when he reminded us that the only thing we have to fear is fear itself. What he might not have expected was that we would still be locked in fear more than 60 years after the end of World War II.

And yet, as a society, we still are. We are currently engaged in a war on terror, which appears to be about as successful as the war on poverty. Who won the war on poverty? Poverty. And what's winning the war on terror? Terror itself.

It's probably just as well that 24-hour news channels, the Internet, and the blogosphere did not exist in FDR's day. We might have been too terrified of the enemy to wage a successful war had our discourse been dominated by the fear mongers and the media. Al-Qaeda attacked us on September 11, 2001, and the news media have attacked us incessantly, on an almost minute-by-minute basis, ever since. So in this chapter, I'd like to talk a little more about conquering fear, because when you know how to kick fear to the curb, you really know how to live.

The first thing to know about fear is that it's not always a bad thing. Sometimes fear is actually our intuition giving us a healthy warning of imminent danger. It can be a sixth sense telling us not to get onto the elevator with the person who looks dangerous or not to go into the empty parking lot late at night. So sometimes fear is a healthy, intuitive response to a dangerous situation. People who sensed in mid-2008 that the stock market was on the brink and sold their holdings can be very grateful for the gift of fear in their lives.

But that's just about the only good thing you can say about fear. Aside from its use as an early warning system, fear is a soul-destroying emotion, something that just sucks the energy and life right out of us. Because of fear, many people won't make commitments in their personal, professional, or economic lives. They're afraid to have children. They're afraid to move. They're afraid to try something new at work. They're afraid to ask someone to marry them, or they're afraid to answer in the affirmative. Many people are afraid to find a new line of work once their old job—or industry—disappears. Truly, there is no single emotion more destructive and incapacitating than fear.

Perhaps the only other useful aspect of fear is if you're afraid of something happening, then it's a good way of knowing that it isn't happening at this moment. Otherwise you wouldn't be in fear of it—it would be happening. But 99 percent of the time, we worry needlessly and fear pointlessly. So how exactly do you conquer fear and recover from its insidious effects?

In order to banish fear, we must call upon yet another angel—in this case, the Guardian Angel of Faith. Faith is the best-known antidote to fear, the means by which we manage stress associated with any sort of fear that may be afflicting us. We've already discussed the importance of opening or strengthening the bond between ourselves and our Higher Power. We need to recognize situations—people, places, and things over which we have no control. We may turn to our Higher Power to handle those situations that seem to be too much for us. In other words, realize that life is such a complicated business that we don't want to go it alone.

So what does it mean to appeal to the Angel of Faith to help eradicate fear? The first step is an admission of powerlessness. Not weakness, but powerlessness—an awareness that it is beyond human power to solve a particular problem. Don't limit the areas in which you're asking for God's help. You can turn to God or your Higher Power for just about every emotional, mental, and social problem that arises in your life. But first you must admit that you cannot solve the problem yourself—especially economic problems in today's world. Next, acknowledge that spiritual help is available. And then ask God, or your Higher Power, to step into the situation and make things right.

You can shorthand this approach to spirituality by saying, "I can't, God can, so I'm going to let God."

Alcoholics Anonymous (A.A.) works because it helps people who fear they have hit bottom and don't want to sink any lower. In today's world, A.A.'s spiritual model works for just about everyone. Many people are suffering because of lost jobs, lost investments, and lost pensions. They're afraid they're going to hit bottom—a one-way trip to the gutter, the poorhouse, whatever metaphor they find most terrifying. There are tens of millions of Americans in panic mode, many of them retirees. They're suffering because of an existential fear of poverty and want. I'm writing specifically for those individuals who need to know that there is hope and there is help. My message is this: You don't have to wait for the economy to turn around before you turn around your own perspective and point of view.

Albert Einstein is credited with saying that the mind that creates a problem is generally not capable of solving that problem for itself. So if our minds become consumed with fear, it's almost too much to ask that our minds bail us out of that problem. Instead, we invite God, or a Higher Power, in to solve the problem for us. "I'm powerless over my fear," you might say. "I know that God has the power to help me.

So I'm going to let Him." This is when you can call on the Angel of Faith to remove your fear and replace it with faith.

Can fear and faith exist side by side in the same mind? Sure. We're humans, after all. So feel the fear and do it anyway. Keep in mind that courage is not the absence of fear; instead, courage is fear that has said its prayers. Although we may be experiencing fear, the simple act of inviting God, or a Higher Power, to remove that fear from us lessens fear's stranglehold on our emotions.

It's also important to remember that even the most successful people in the world experienced tons of fear before they accomplished great things. They simply didn't let the fear hold them back. For example, Bill Russell, one of the greatest basketball players in history, was said to throw up before every single game. His level of fear was enormous... but so were his talent and drive. He never let his fear get in the way of his success.

There may be some individuals who have been able to succeed without experiencing any fear at all, but they are exceptions to the rule. Most people, no matter how talented or confident, still experience fear. It's said that all good public speaking is born of fear. Many public speakers will tell you that if they don't feel fear prior to ascending the speaker's platform, then they have *real* reason to fear—because they know they won't do a good job!

Another thing to consider with fear is that it's a part of us, and so it need not be attacked or destroyed in order for us to be comfortable. The wisest among us embrace or at least accept their dark sides—the negative aspects of their personalities—instead of trying to isolate or eliminate them. So perhaps we're asking for the impossible when we say we want to eliminate fear from our lives. Instead, perhaps the appropriate goal is to eliminate fear's corrosive, toxic, destructive tendencies from our thought patterns and mindset so we can go out and accomplish everything that our heart desires.

So what do we do with fear? People usually want to fix it fast. That can't be done, because first we have to notice it without judgment; that is, the economy is what it is, so we need to stop being angry, resentful, or victimized by it, because that just adds fuel to the fear. The first thing to do is NOTHING! It's tough because we usually say, "Don't just stand there, do something." But first we have to hit the pause button to notice it, get our arms around it, and then be free to act on it without obsessing over it.

I have a patient who says, "I'm scared all the time because I always show myself scary movies in my head." Get your focus off scary thoughts by doing things that nourish you: walking in nature, listening to soothing music, meditation, movies, seeing friends. Even a fresh apple can do the trick, so go to a farmer's market and get a delicious, organic, locally grown one. Ask yourself: What can I do that nourishes me? This triggers a chemical reaction and life energy flow in the brain and body, and this can dissolve your fear. In other words, accentuate the positive...and stay there.

Once you do the above, then you can more effectively attend seminars, polish your résumé, go job hunting, and so on. Only then can real problem solving be done.

Obsessing people often dismiss as pointless the very things that would help them by saying, "Why in the world am I taking a walk when I should be searching for a job, not entertaining myself?" Or you might think, "I don't want to call and connect with my friend and bother him," even though that's exactly what would help free you from fear. Actually, the walk or the call would be releasing and generating life energy. These actions will change body and brain chemistry to dampen fear and make you more ready to join the work force again.

What does it mean to replace fear with faith, especially in troubled economic times like these? It really means that we attain a new level of freedom in our lives, because fear holds us back from taking chances and making choices. As Swiss psychiatrist Carl Jung wrote, "I am not what happened to me...I am what I choose to become." Once we can let the fear go, once we can find a path to action that is not hobbled by fear, we can do just about anything. The surprising fact about faith is that it lacks permanence. We might expect that once we have achieved a level of faith, we will never experience fear again, as if faith were some sort of mental martial art in which we can be awarded a black belt that is ours forever. Actually, faith is a lot more like vitamin C—it needs to be replenished on a daily basis. So don't be surprised if you take the steps I suggest here to eliminate the effects of fear from your life only to see it return the next day. That's simply how we humans appear to be wired.

Why is faith so important? Why is it such a powerful antidote to fear? Perhaps the ultimate purpose of fear is to give us the opportunity to reconnect with God, or a Higher Power, on a regular basis. If we were never in fear, we would never need to look beyond ourselves, and we might miss our true purpose in life, which is to love God and serve people, and to love people and serve God. Perhaps that is the true gift of fear—it creates opportunities in our lives to pause, to reflect, and to reach out to something greater than ourselves.

Humans are hardwired to pay attention to fear (again, think about the concept of survival of the fittest). Imagine a beautiful day in central Africa at the dawn of civilization. We see an example of Early Man gazing around him with wonder and awe at the natural world that surrounds him. He may lack the language to express his feelings, but he is moved and pleased by the beauty of the flawless blue sky, the green hills, and the trees. Off in the distance, he hears a faint rumbling sound.

He turns and sees a cloud of dust perhaps a mile away. Suddenly everything changes for this individual. His breathing goes shallow, and he focuses intently on that cloud of dust and the threat it most likely represents. What he is seeing is a predatory animal, and either he or it will be lunch for the other. At this moment, he is no longer interested in the beautiful sky, the green hills, or anything other than survival.

Fast forward to the present moment. How different are we from that unsophisticated ancestor of ours whom we just met? Ninety percent of our lives could be working perfectly—we're healthy; we have love in our life; we have a job, food and shelter; we have a car. We have all the necessities and many of the luxuries that even kings from hundreds of years ago could never have imagined in their own lives. And yet, what do we focus on? The 90 percent of our lives that is running smoothly? Or the 10 percent, the cloud of dust?

Today, however, the percentages seem to be reversed. Ninety percent of our lives—finances, health, relationships—are in crisis, and the cloud of dust seems more like an enveloping fog.

But we must remember that there is no predator charging toward us through that cloud of dust. All there is... is dust. Empty fear and no more. We'll survive the economic downturn. We may be tightening our belts, witnessing a reduction or loss of income, and yes, unfortunately, some individuals have lost their homes. So what can we do right now to improve our frame of mind while we're waiting for the economy to turn around? How can we face life's challenges with a positive mindset when so much of the news is so negative? We can take advantage of the fact that humans are also hardwired to have faith. Faith is a major element of how the fittest have survived.

It is human nature to concentrate on what makes us afraid, to the exclusion of all else in our lives. For this reason, one of the most powerful tools for eliminating fear is the concept of gratitude.

It is all but impossible to be grateful and fearful at the same time. The next time you find yourself experiencing fear, invite your mind to create a short list of things for which you are grateful—your life, your health, your faith, your family, your friends, your job, your children, your grandchildren. But the most important thing is that you make that list. Gratitude has a wondrous power to dispel fear. When we think of the things that bring us true happiness, it's hard to stay locked into thinking about the things that cause us upset. When we cultivate the attitude of gratitude, when we make that mental or, even better, written list of things that bring us joy, we shift the mind from a stance of "what if," "what if," "what if?" to a state of appreciation of "what is," what is," what is." We need to stop thinking of what we've lost and instead focus on what we have. And there are few more powerful shifts that the mind can make.

Here is a practical application of this approach to conquering fear. Instead of allowing our minds to ask, "What if I lose my job?" a better question to focus on would be, "What kind of training or connections would make me more valuable to my current employer or to other employers in today's job market?"

The Buddhists teach that the mind is like a chariot—it can pull us in any direction, or we can exert control over it and have it take us where we want to go. Fear leads that chariot astray. Gratitude gets it back on the right course.

The Angel of Faith is standing by, awaiting your call, to remove fear from your mindset. Let Her.

*

TO CALL ON THE GUARDIAN ANGEL OF FAITH...

When your problems are simply too big to solve without help, acknowledge that spiritual help is available for coping with fear. Invite your Higher Power to come into your life to solve the problem. Cultivate an attitude of gratitude, and move from the upsetting memories of what you've lost to the realization of what you still have. And get ready to find that when a problem arises, the solution may be an angel in human form!

CHAPTER 9

HARNESSING THE TRUE POWER OF THE MIND

If your mind is out to get you, then you have a very small
and insignificant enemy!

—ANONYMOUS

What's worse, physical illness or emotional illness?

As a physician, I find that a very difficult question to answer. Most physical illnesses, fortunately, can be cured today, except for most of the autoimmune diseases, such as cancer, in which the body essentially attacks itself. Emotional illness could be viewed in much the same light—it is a situation where the mind turns against its owner, like a cancer of the mind. It creates an inaccurate world view so upsetting and depressing that the only logical course, in extreme cases, is suicide.

In this chapter, I'd like to introduce you to the Guardian Angel of Truth. She is standing by, ready for your call, to help you make the most of the strength that your mind possesses.

Fortunately, the power of the mind to create is just as strong as its power to destroy. I want to share with you five vital ways in which you can use the power of your mind to eliminate stress from your life and in so doing provide you with the satisfaction and joy that life truly has to offer. So let's dive right in.

Realize that you are part of something greater.

Our technology- and success-driven society places so much emphasis on the individual that we have forgotten some of the most basic truths about human existence. Just as the wave draws its beauty and power from the fact that it belongs to the ocean, so do we human beings derive our core identity and meaning from the fact that we are part of a collective that is so much greater than any one individual. I love what Mahatma Gandhi said of human beings: "What you do is insignificant, but it is essential that you do it."

It's easy for us to feel discouraged, to feel that our lives or efforts don't matter. But they do! Each of us was created for a reason, and each of us has a uniqueness that no other human being can match. To put it simply, no other person could play the role that you and only you are destined to play. No one else could raise your children as well. No one else could be a friend like you. No one else could be you as well as you. In the Jewish Talmud, the rabbis make an intriguing comment about the difference between a mortal king on the one hand and God on the other. When a mortal king, the rabbis write, places his image on a coin, every single coin bearing his image is identical to all the rest. And yet, when the king of kings, God, places his image on a human being, it is different from all the rest. That's how much greater God is than any mortal king, and that demonstrates your uniqueness, your importance, and the responsibility each of us bears to play our part in life. Also in the Talmud, a Rabbi Zuschia says to God, "I am not nearly as great a Torah scholar as is Rabbi Hillel or Rabbi Akiva. Why am I even here?"

To which God replies, "Don't worry about them. I created you to be the best possible Rabbi Zuschia."

And so it is with us. Meaning is not something readily evident in the day-to-day activities in which we engage—getting a child fed and dressed for school, handling difficult problems at work, even singing in the church choir. It is up to us to find the meaning in what we do. There's the story about the three men who are digging a ditch in the hot sun. Someone came up to them and asked, "What are you guys doing?"

The first man answered, "I'm digging a ditch."

The second man replied, "I'm making $12 an hour."

The third individual answered, "I'm building a cathedral."

Enough said.

Be ethical and contribute.

An ongoing debate in American life is the extent to which the private lives of public figures should be made public. If the President of the United States is having an affair with a subordinate, is that something we need to know? And whether we need to know it or not, does it affect his ability to serve as President?

I'm not going to wade into that debate, because the purpose of this book is spiritual rather than political in nature. But I will say this: It is impossible for us to be our best selves if we are violating our own ethical norms. That's true whether we are President of the United States or unemployed. As we've discussed earlier, it takes enormous energy—life energy— to live in a manner that violates our beliefs about how we should live. Keeping secrets requires enormous energy, as we have discussed, and the other side of the coin is that we must find ways to justify our behavior to ourselves. Every good deed draws in its wake another good deed, and every wrong or impure act draws in its wake another impure or negative act. So the question is, Who do we really want to be—an individual suffused with guilt, who gets caught up in behavior patterns that eventually seem almost impossible to break, or an individual living in concert with his or her values.

Pop quiz: What group of people in our society are portrayed as the bad guys more than any other on TV crime dramas, year after year after year?

The surprising answer: Business people.

People in business are frequently portrayed in popular culture as villains. As events leading up to the current economic crisis indicate, sometimes that disdainful view of business people is entirely justified. But the reality is that for every banker or subprime mortgage lender or Ponzi scheme operator whose actions contributed to the economic meltdown, there are thousands and even millions of business people who lead honest, decent lives at work and away from work, and whose efforts make possible all of the products and services that enhance our lives. The reason our society is so strong is that there are so many people in the arena of business and labor who do provide an honest day's work for a day's pay, who design and build our communities and our homes, who create our automobiles, who invent the technological devices like BlackBerrys and iPhones that we all but take for granted in today's world, who create the TV shows, movies, and video games that offer us decent entertainment, and so on.

All we hear about, however, are the bad apples, the ones whose greed overwhelms their sense of morality. It's just as true in politics as it is in any other field—it never makes news when someone does the right thing. I bring this up because in an era like ours, it seems as though the most successful people—and the ones who "got away with it"— are the ones who cheated. That's not true now, nor has it ever been true. When we are ethical and we make our own unique contributions to society, we are using our minds in the way they are meant to be used, and we avoid the mental conflict that inevitably accompanies our lives when we color outside the lines.

What goes around comes around.

In the West, we call it the Golden Rule: Do unto others as you would have them do unto you. In the East, they call it karma. It seems that one thing upon which practically the whole world agrees is that as we act, so the world will act toward us. It may not seem true in every case, and in this lifetime we may never solve the problem of why bad things happen to good people. If we are deserving of good things, good things will come to us.

It's impossible to plant fruit and get vegetables. As we sow, we reap. This is an immutable law of the universe. The great motivator Earl Nightingale said that the universe does not play favorites—it treats each of us based on our behavior, not on our social position, wealth, or standing. If we expect that we are going to get away with something, we're setting ourselves up for disappointment, failure, and even tragedy. This is not how the world works, and deep down, we all know that. The good news is that the Golden Rule, or the Law of Karma, allows each of us a wonderful source of power in our lives. We cannot control the actions of others, but by monitoring and being responsible for our actions, we create the karma we need for a successful life. You might ask, "If that's true, then how come all the people I know who do the wrong thing really do seem to get away with it?"

My response to that question is that what goes around comes around—sometimes sooner, sometimes later—but it always works that way. As the expression goes, Everything is okay in the end, and if it's not okay…then it's not the end!

Find the strength to overcome adversity.

Motivational author Zig Ziglar wrote that he wished he could sell us our brains for $100,000 each. That way, we would actually value our brains…and he would have $100,000.

The sad reality is that we put little value on that which comes to us for free. Even the best research scientists have never been able to create a computer that approximates even to the slightest degree the complexity, flexibility, and computing capacity of the human brain. You can teach a computer to play chess, but you cannot teach a computer to love. You may be able to access the Internet from your cell phone, but your cell phone will never be able to create a symphony. (At least not one I want to listen to.) At the outset of this chapter, we discussed the power of the mind to destroy, to convince us that all is lost, that all is hopeless, and that there is no reason for going on. This is the mindset that leads to depression, despair, and perhaps, ultimately, suicide.

At the same time, the power of the mind to destroy, as we also discussed, is, in my opinion, minuscule compared to its power to solve problems, to find answers, and to overcome adversity. The brain is a question-answering machine. Ask it a poorly constructed question, and you'll get a bad result. "Why does everything go wrong in my life?"

The brain will think and think and think until it comes up with a suitable answer: "Because you're a failure!"

So if you want your mind to produce better answers, ask better questions.

"How can I solve this problem?"

"How can I create a better situation for myself and my loved ones?"

"How can I earn more money?"

"How can I create a better future for my children?"

In other words, you can use your mind to confront adversity head on (no pun intended). As Shakespeare wrote, you can "take arms against a sea of troubles, and by opposing, end them." This is a wonderful use of the mind, and it all comes down to asking better questions. Human beings have overcome all manner of adversity and misery, including periods of time that make our economic struggles look like a walk in the park. This is why friends and support groups are so important—it can be extremely helpful to know that we are not the only ones suffering in a certain way. The collective wisdom of friends or a group in such situations, whether face to face or online, is astonishing. Don't be afraid to use your mind to seek out solutions to even the most vexing of life's problems. You truly have the strength to overcome adversity if you would only tap into that great strength.

Have the courage to create.

When Beethoven sat down to write his magnificent Fifth Symphony, he had no guarantee that the piece of music bouncing around in his head would become one of the most beloved of all time and would long outlive him. Did Shakespeare know that audiences would be moved by the dramatization of the story of Othello, either in his day or hundreds of years later? When parents have their first child, they have no guarantees about how the whole thing is going to turn out. Whether we are creating a symphony or a child, we need courage.

And if we look to the Angel of Truth, we will find that courage deep inside us. There are no guarantees in this life. No promises, no sure things. There's a scene in the classic comedy film *When Harry Met Sally*, in which we learn that Harry likes to read the last few pages of a book before he begins. He finds great comfort and solace in knowing how things are going to turn out. It might be an effective life skill for a neurotic single guy, but that's not the way life really works.

Everything in life takes courage. The good news is that you have been gifted at birth, and at no charge, with the most wondrous creation the world has ever known—the human mind. You received a trillion-dollar thinking apparatus for free, and along with it comes the biblical injunction: To whom much is given, much is expected. Have the courage to create in your life, whether you are creating a home, a business, supper, or a string quartet. Look around us, and all you see is creation—in a sunrise, a tree, a formation of birds, a body of water. We are meant to imitate a creative, loving God. And our mind is the primary tool by which we create and shape our world.

It's hard to remain stressed when you're absorbed in the challenge to create, to build, and to serve.

So there you have it—five powerful ways to harness the power of your mind to alleviate the crippling effects of stress and allow you to be, to do, to have, and to create all that is in your power. To go back to the Buddhist teaching for a moment, your mind is that extraordinarily powerful chariot. Where do you want to go today?

*

TO CALL ON THE GUARDIAN ANGEL OF TRUTH...

Recognize that you are part of something greater in your own life. Find purpose and meaning in who you are and what you do. Be ethical and contribute to society. Live by the Golden Rule. Find the strength to overcome adversity by inviting your mind to ask better questions in order to solve the problems you may face. It has been said that God gives every bird its food, but He does not throw it into the nest. Have the courage to create, because the world is full of talented people who never found the courage to use their talent to make the world a better place. It's hard to stay stressed-out when you're using your mind in such powerful ways.

CHAPTER 10

IT'S STILL AMERICA, AND YOU'RE STILL YOU!

The future's so bright, I gotta wear shades!

—'80S ROCK GROUP TIMBUK3

Get ready for our nation's recovery, because America is going to come back bigger and stronger than ever. Perhaps we'll have learned some lessons from the errors and miscalculations of the last decade so that we'll not only be stronger but also wiser in the choices we make in our economy and in our relations with the rest of the world. (That's about as political as I'm going to get.) I truly believe that our nation will come back not just bigger, stronger, and wiser, but more spiritual than ever before.

Our economy has been based on consumption—conspicuous, mindless, and fueled by cheap credit. Perhaps we will be more oriented as a result of our experience in this time of economic uncertainty to be less interested in things and more interested in people and the realm of the spirit.

Minister Cecil "Chip" Murray used to preach that "Small minds talk about people. Average minds talk about events. Great minds talk about ideas." Perhaps our society will emerge from this period of war and economic confusion with its spirituality strengthened with an appropriate dash of humility. Young people who have never been through an economic downturn before might easily assume, from viewing news reports of the economy, that the sky has fallen and that the economy will never recover.

Older folks, who have been through a downturn or two, might watch the news and feel the same way. But you and I are now schooled in a different way of thinking. We recognize that downturns are temporary, but the realm of the spirit lives forever. Stress, which we have equated with fear, may have seemed like an impossible enemy to overcome. But even in the time it's taken you to read these pages, I hope that you have found some effective ways to eliminate some of the harms and dangers of stress from your life.

That's why I say that America is still America, and you're still you, bigger, stronger, more powerful, and more spiritual than ever before. When you knock stress out of the equation, life takes on new beauty, meaning, and purpose. You can keep stress at bay, no matter what's happening on the outside, by learning how to feel worthy of your own love, the love of others, and of your Creator, too.

You get that by living the way you know you're supposed to live and by nurturing your body, your mind, and your spirit in the ways that I have outlined. Then you can experience the peace, grace, and hope that make life the beautiful adventure we all deserve.

These are crazy times. Entire industries, from retail to banking, from auto manufacturing to real estate, are in upheaval and are likely to emerge from this period in a different form from anything we have known before. This is indeed a time of great uncertainty, compounded by the media's exaggerations and fear inducing tactics. I wrote this book as a counterweight to the bad news that seemingly every American absorbs on a daily basis, even those whose jobs, lives, and finances are reasonably secure.

I'm reminded that the Chinese symbol for crisis is also the symbol for opportunity, and I see enormous opportunity in this time for us as individuals, and for our society as a whole, to shift our consciousness to a more spiritual plane. In order to do so, however, we need to be cognizant of the effects of stress, and we need down-to-earth, sensible, easy-to-implement solutions to the problems we face.

Throughout this book, I have called on angels, because they are a universally understood and even beloved expression of God's love and grace. Again, I was inspired by Abraham Lincoln's appeal to call upon our "better angels." Now I'd like to introduce you to the last angel we'll call upon in this book—you, yourself.

My purpose in writing has been to give you an awareness of the power you possess to grow metaphorical wings and soar over the day-to-day stresses of modern life.

As your own angel, you become your own primary care physician, because you have been empowered in these pages with the tools you need in order to take the best possible care of yourself physically, mentally, and spiritually. You now realize how much your health is determined not by chance or by medicine but by personal responsibility, self-value, and reverence for life.

As your own angel, you are now a world-class lifestyle coach, purely by adapting, in stages or all at once, the simple approach to nutrition and exercise that I've shared with you.

As your own angel, you are now the most powerful teacher you will ever encounter, because you now know how to harness the power of your mind to take you in directions that will maximize your own personal fulfillment and your own unique contribution to society.

And as your own angel, you can now serve yourself as the best possible therapist, recognizing stressful or destructive thoughts and actions and replacing them with healthier ones.

Angels live to love and serve. That is their sole mission on Earth. If you glance down, you might just see wings that you never knew you possessed. Try them out. Fly. Coast on a jet stream and see the intricacy and beauty of your life from an entirely different perspective. It's said that if we stand too close to a painting, all we see are brushstrokes that appear random. But when we step back, we see a beautiful portrait, landscape, or other recognizable image.

So it is with the perspective we gain from the angels we've called upon, and now from our own role as angels. Your life looks different from up on high, doesn't it? I'm sure it does. I'm sure it looks more beautiful than ever. As an angel, you are now charged with the delightful responsibility of sharing your gift of love and service, peace and tranquillity, harmony and spirituality with the world in desperate need for those gifts. Those have been the gifts that I've sought to share with you, and I look forward to hearing from you and discovering how you have applied them in your own life and how you have brought your own angelic grace to touch the lives of those you love. Thank you for allowing me to be with you on this part of your life's journey, and henceforth, when I call on all angels, I'll be calling on you!

EPILOGUE

Dr. Taub's
Emergency Stress Meditations

At the back of the book, we have included a CD of meditations. Before you begin a meditation, please listen to the suggestions at the beginning of each meditation track. Or if you prefer, ask someone else to slowly read the meditation to you. Once you become familiar with the meditation, find a comfortable spot, and practice the meditation by yourself.

****

FOR PEACE OF MIND IN YOUR LIFE,
IT'S IMPORTANT TO MEDITATE EVERY DAY.

MEDITATION REMINDS YOU OF YOUR INNER STRENGTH:
YOUR HIGHER POWER, GOD, YOUR GUARDIAN ANGELS.

YOU'LL BEGIN BY TAKING LONG, DEEP, EVEN BREATHS,
WHILE RELAXING ALL THE MUSCLES OF YOUR BODY.

THEN YOU'LL IMAGINE A WARM, HEALING LIGHT,
FILLING YOUR HEART AND YOUR ENTIRE BODY.

Epilogue

AFTER YOU BECOME FILLED WITH LIGHT,
THEN YOU WILL ACTUALLY BECOME THE LIGHT.

IF YOUR THOUGHTS INTRUDE WHILE YOU ARE MEDITATING,
JUST SAY THE FOLLOWING WORDS SILENTLY, OVER AND OVER:
"I HAVE STRENGTH...I HAVE STRENGTH...I HAVE STRENGTH."

****

- Close your eyes and take a long, deep breath, and as you let it out, relax the muscles of your face...including the muscles behind your eyes and at the base of your tongue.

- Take another long, deep breath, and as you let it out, relax the muscles of your neck, shoulders, arms, forearms, and fingers.

- Take another long, deep breath, and as you let it out, relax the muscles of your chest, your abdomen, and your back...just relax.

- Take another long, deep breath, and as you let it out, relax the muscles of your buttocks, thighs, calves, feet, and toes...just relax.

- Continue breathing, and imagine a warm, healing golden light filling your entire heart with warmth and healing and love.

- Now imagine the warm, healing, golden light radiating gently outward from your heart to fill your entire body:

  ...filling your abdomen, pelvis, legs, feet, and toes—with light.

  ...filling your chest, neck, shoulders, and arms—down to your fingertips.

  ...filling your mouth, nose, eyes, ears, and brain...so your entire body and mind become filled with warm, healing golden light.

- Now imagine the golden light becoming so pure and so intense that you actually become the light. Allow yourself to become the light.

- Silently say the following three words to yourself, over and over, for as long as you wish...or just enjoy being quiet and still...until you wish to open your eyes:

  "I have strength...I have strength...I have strength...I have strength..."

Note: If you would like, substitute another phrase or mantra for "I have strength":

"God loves me...God loves me...God loves me."

Or...

"I love you, God...I love you, God...I love you, God...I love you, God..."

INDEX

A

addiction, 47
adrenal glands, 54
alcohol, 3, 80
Alcoholics Anonymous (A.A.), 47–49,
    84, 96. *See also* Higher Power
Allen, James, 75
altruism, benefits of, 87
America, 3, 115–19
    health care system in, ix, 10, 61-62
    myths of, 7–9
Angel(s), viii, 6, 11-12, 118-19
    of Compassion, 90, 92
    of Faith, 95, 103
    of Health, 61, 67
    of Hope, 12–13
    of Love, 32, 38
    of Peace, 21, 23–25
    of Strength, 42, 55
    of Time, 81–82
    of Truth, 105, 113, 114
anti-acid medications, 61–62

B

behavior
    altruistic, 87
    children's, 3

    ethical, 45–47, 107–89
    negative, 47
    "Type A," 11, 70–71
breathing, stress and, 52
Browning, Robert, 50
business people as villains, 108–9

C

caffeine, 80
calorie counting, 65
carbohydrates, 63, 64
cardiovascular benefits of walking, 44
change, accepting, 17
charitable giving, 87
clutter, 77–78
commercial marketing of medications,
    61–62
communication. *See also* connection
    to others
    marriage and, 34
    technology and, 22, 71
Compassion, Angel of, 90, 92
"compassion fatigue," 90–91
computers. *See* technology
competition in schools and workplace,
    stress of, 22

Index

conflict, 3
connection to others, 81, 84–85
  distractions from, 29–30, 33–35
  intimacy, 36-37, 85
cortisol, 54
courage, 112–13
creativity, 112–13

D

danger warning system, 94
depression, 3
dietary supplements, 66–67
dieting, 65
disease, vi, vii, 2, 105. *See also* health
distractions from family, 29–30
distress, 17
divorce, 3, 31–32. *See also* marriage
domestic stressors, 2–3. *See also* specific
    kinds
drug abuse, 3

E

Eagleton, Tom, 8–9
eating right, 57–67
economic stressors, x, 1–2, 27–29
  two-worker family, 31
economy, 4, 115
  money-related stressors, 1-2
eggs, 63
Einstein, Albert, 96
emotional illness, 105
empty nesters, stresses on, 27–28
environment, control over, 78
ethical behavior, 45–47, 107–9
eu-stress, 17
exercise, 43–44
  impersonal love and, 87
external circumstances, stress
    management and, x, 13, 41–55

F

faith. *See also* God; Higher Power;
    spirituality
  Angel of, 95, 103
  importance of, 100–2
family, 27–38
  dinner, 33–34, 38
  distractions from, 29–30
  importance of, 35
  stresses on, 27–32
  throwaway marriage, 31–32
  two-worker, 31
  youth as commodity, 30
fear, 93–103
fish, 63
"flight or fight," 18
foods
  healthy, 60–61
  "live" vs. "dead," 62–63
  myths about, 64–66
Fox, Michael J., x
Friedman, Meyer, 11
friends, importance of, 112
fruits, 63, 65

G

Gandhi, Mahatma, 106
God, 95–96. *See also* faith; Higher
    Power
  absence of, fear and, 93
  connection to, viii, 47–49
Golden Rule, 110
gratitude, 102
greed, 109
Guardian Angels, viii, 6, 11-12, 118-19
  Angel of Compassion, 90, 92
  Angel of Faith, 95, 103
  Angel of Health, 61, 67
  Angel of Hope, 12–13
  Angel of Love, 32, 38

Index

Angel of Peace, 21, 23–25
Angel of Strength, 42, 55
Angel of Time, 81–82
Angel of Truth, 105, 113, 114
guilt, 108

H
health, vi
  altruism and, 87
  Angel of, 61, 67
  emotional illness and, 105
  "hurry sickness," 70-71, 72
  love and, 84
  maximizing, 5
  medications, 61-62
  meditation and, 51–52
  multitasking and, 77
  physical illness and, 105
  sleep and, 79–80
  stress and, vii, 7
  "Type A behavior" and, 11, 70–71
health care in the U.S., ix, 10, 61–62
healthy foods, 60–61
Higher Power, 6, 47–49, 95–96. *See
    also* faith; God
  lack of belief in, fear and, 93
home
  peaceful environment in, 77–78
  as source of stress, 28–32
Hope, Angel of, 12–13
hormones, stress, 54
"Hour of Power" TV show, xi
"hurry sickness," 70–71, 72

I
illness, vi, vii, 2, 105. *See also* health
  spiritual, 11
impersonal love, 86–92
information, speed of, 22
intimacy, 36-37, 85

J
John Wayne personality type, 7–8
Jung, Carl, 99

K
Karma, Law of, 110

L
laughter, 54
Law of Karma, 110
Leary, Timothy, 33
legumes, 63
life, meaning of, 107
Lincoln, Abraham, 11, 117
loneliness, 35, 84, 88, 89
love
  Angel of, 32, 38
  expressing in marriage, 36–37
  health and, 84
  impersonal, 86-92

M
Maimonides, 87
managing stress
  exercise and, 43–44
  nutrition and, 57–67
  time management and, 69–82
marketing of medications, 61-62
marriage
  communication and, 34
  divorce, 3, 31–32
  intimacy in, 36–37
meaning of life, 107
media, 13
  stress and, 4, 29–30
  television, 32-34, 73
  tuning out, 13, 38, 73
medical system in the U.S., ix, 10,
    61-62
medications, anti-acid, 61–62

Index

meditation, 49–53
mentoring, 86
milk, 65
money-related stressors, 1–2
Montesquieu, Baron de, 86
morality, 45–47, 107-9
movement as exercise, 44
multitasking, 76–77
Murray, Cecil "Chip," 116
myths
    American, 7-9
    food, 64–66

N
naps, 81
neatness, 78
negative statements, avoiding, 74–75
negative stress, 17
news, tuning out, 13, 32–34, 38
Nicklaus, Jack, 9
nicotine, 80
Nightingale, Earl, 24, 110
nutrition, 57–67
nutritional supplements, 66–67

O
obesity, 2. *See also* overweight
O'Connor, Donald, 16
overweight, 2, 57–58

P
parents, 27, 71. *See also* families
Peace, Angel of, 21, 23–25
Peale, Norman Vincent, 83–84
personal affronts, 71
personality type, John Wayne, 7–8
personal love, 86
physiological response to impersonal
    love, 87
Plato, xi

pleasure, importance of, 53–54
portion control, 66
positive stress, 17
positive thinking, 5, 7, 74–75
poultry, 63
powerlessness, awareness of, 95–96
power of the mind, 105–14
prayer, 49–53
prescription drugs, ix
preventive medicine, ix
prioritizing, 76–78

R
reality, 4
response to stress, x, 6
rest, importance of, 79–80
retirees, 27–28
road rage, 71
Roosevelt, Franklin Delano, 93
Rosenman, Ray H., 11
routine, breaking up, 81
Russell, Bill, 97

S
Sabbath, 80
Schuller, Robert H., xi
secrets, 108
Selye, Hans, 17
service to others, 86–92
Shakespeare, William, 112
Singing in the Rain, 16
sleep, importance of, 79–80
smiling, 54, 81
snacking, 63–65
speed of information, 22
spiritual illness, 11
spirituality, 10, 95–96. *See also* faith;
    God; Higher Power
    connection to God, 47–49
Strength, Angel of, 42, 55

stress
    biological, 17
    defined, 15–20
    effects of, 7, 20
    external circumstances and, 41–55
    families and, 27–32
    hormones, 54
    managing, 39–55
    negative, 17
    positive, 17
    response to, 17–18
    as spiritual illness, 10
    technology and, 21–22
stressors, x, 1-3, 27-29, 31
sunshine, importance of, 45
support groups, importance of, 112

T
Talmud, Jewish, 6, 7, 106–7
tea drinking, 54
technology, 13
    communication and, 71
    stress and, 21–22, 29–30
    turning it off in the home, 32–34,
        38, 73
television, 13, 32–34, 73
theodicy, 48
time
    Angel of, 81–82
    lack of, 69–82
tragedy, 48–49
transportation, 21-22
Truth, Angel of, 105, 113, 114

Twain, Mark, 45
two-worker family, 31
"Type A behavior," 11, 70-71

V
vacations, 81
vegetables, 63
violence, sports and, 71
Vitamin D, 45
vitamin supplements, 66–67
volunteering, 86

W
walking, benefits of, 44
water, importance of, 64
weight loss, 65
weight training, 44
wellness, x. See also health
Western medicine, 10
Woods, Tiger, 9
work
    boundaries of, 69–70
    ethical behavior and, 108–9
    two-worker family, 31
world view, 4, 7–8

Y
youth as commodity, 30

Z
Ziglar, Zig, 111
Zuschia, Rabbi, 107

ACKNOWLEDGMENTS

David Oliphant and Deborah A. Kalman are the best friends and partners that a mere human being could ask for. I am humbled.

Michael Levin is a superb craftsman, who has taught me a great deal about the art of writing. I am thankful.

QVC has given me the opportunity to practice Integrative Medicine with total conscience and dignity, and Dr. James Rouse has given this book his unflagging support, for which I am grateful.

Dr. Wil Smith enriched my insight into human emotions.

My wife, Anneli Taub, is my Angel. I am blessed.

— *Edward A. Taub, M.D., FAAP*

****

I acknowledge my mentors Milton Dicus, Charles Monahan, John Robinson, Bob Saffi, and the men of the Westside.

—*Michael Levin*

****

Acknowledgments

First, I want to acknowledge Deborah A. Kalman for her incredible support, hard work, love, and dedication to this project. Actually, she should have been listed as a coauthor for the invaluable, intelligent contributions she has made to this book.

Second, and equally important, is my tremendous respect and appreciation for the Reader's Digest team, headed by Harold Clarke, president and publisher of Reader's Digest Trade Publishing, who is one of the finest, most knowledgeable, caring, and honest publishers I have known in my 50 years in the publishing industry, on every level. He is truly a refreshing leader in this era of lost entrepreneurialism in our treasured publishing industry.

This acknowledgment would not be complete if I didn't give a special shout-out to Dianne Barnum, Harold's administrative assistant, whom I have grown to greatly respect. This book could not have been completed and published without her intelligence, dedication, and tireless assistance. Thank you for everything.

Dolores York is the ultimate professional, and a delight to work with. Her cooperation and genuine caring truly made the publishing of this book seamless.

To complete the Reader's Digest team, we want to thank Senior Art Director George McKeon for all the work he did so beautifully on this project.

A special thank you to QVC, Inc., the greatest company in the world to work with. It's nice to be able to say that and mean it after 20 years. With special appreciation to Doug Howe, John Kelly, Rich Yoegel, Jessica Lesko, and Dana Bing for supporting this book and helping to make it happen.

Finally, my acknowledgment and thanks must go to my coauthors who have been on the fast track, have tolerated all my demands, and delivered. Both Edward A. Taub, M.D., FAAP, and Michael Levin are extraordinarily brilliant professionals, and most important, genuinely real and caring people.

—David Oliphant